PREFACE TO FIRST EDITION

This book is designed to meet the needs of pupils studying modern British social and economic history at C.S.E. level. The main developments since 1700 are outlined and particular attention has been paid to those features of the contemporary social scene which we take for granted but which are the end point of a period of rapid change.

The illustrations for the book have been chosen with great care, many of them have not been reproduced before in books designed for use in schools, and the authors are particularly grateful for the help received from their publishers in this connection. Much valuable information can be obtained from a study of the pictures and readers are encouraged to use them fully rather than regarding them as mere decoration.

The book is divided into five main sections each of which can be used as a basis for project and topic work. Section 5, which attempts to explain the origins of many current social trends, should be particularly valuable as a starting point for discussions.

There is much dispute at present in academic circles about the whole field of modern social and economic history. Different historians have interpreted the evidence on such topics as the agricultural changes of the eighteenth century and living standards in the early nineteenth century in widely different ways. While the authors have been aware of this, they have also been conscious that a textbook at this level must present its readers with conclusions and a middle road has therefore been taken wherever possible between the extremes of academic controversy.

In the final analysis all History is concerned with people and the authors have tried to keep their approach to the social and economic changes of the last 275 years an essentially 9uman one.

S. L. C.
D. J. H.

PREFACE TO SECOND EDITION

Since this book was first published in 1971, Britain has joined the European Economic Community and has also carried out considerable exploitation of her oil resources in the North Sea. The opportunity has therefore been taken to bring up to date the story of Britain's long struggle to regain economic well being, although inevitably this section of the book lacks a conclusion.

Historians have yet to reach definitive views of earlier episodes in our history. The authors have striven to maintain the balance of the first edition in those areas where controversy has been most protracted. The chapter dealing with the Agricultural Revolution acknowledges the view that Tull and Townshend are not the pioneers that they were once thought to be.

A new edition has presented an opportunity to go metric, although in a number of cases the old and the new measuring scales have been given. The authors feel that older pupils may still be undergoing a process of adjustment.

S.L.C.
D.J.H.

ACKNOWLEDGMENTS

We would like to thank the following for permission to reproduce the photographs, portraits, prints and drawings in this book:

Aerofilms Ltd. (110, 118 bottom, 138 bottom)
British Aircraft Corp. (128 bottom)
B.B.C. (129 bottom)
British Leyland Motor Corp. (100)
British Museum (124 top)
British Railways (61 top, 62 bottom)
British Steel Corp. (76 bottom)
British Transport Museum, Clapham (60 centre, 62 top)
Central Office of Information (132 bottom)
Common Ground (25 bottom)
Department of Planning & Development, Teeside (123 bottom)
Ford of Britain (126)
Fox Photos Ltd. (103)
John Freeman (40, 49)
G.L.C. (118 top)
Guy's Hospital (137)
Handley Page (127 bottom)
Hoover Ltd. (117 left)
Imperial Chemical Industries Ltd. (131)
Imperial War Museum (109)
Labour Party Library (102)
Leeds Central Libraries (117 right, 119, 121)
Lever Brothers Ltd. (23, 74, 116 top)
Liverpool City Libraries (58)
London Electrotype Agency (90)
London Transport Executive (93 top, 129 top)
Manchester Public Libraries (72, 83 bottom, 84 top, 85 bottom)
Mansell Collection (16 left, 43, 45, 46 top, 55, 57, 64 bottom, 77, 80 bottom, 84 bottom)
Hugh McNight (33)
Mitchell Library, Glasgow (98)
National Portrait Gallery (11 right, 71)
Paul Perry (103 top)
Popperfoto (113)
Peter Joslin (132 top)
Post Office Headquarters (7 top)
Radio Times Hulton Picture Library (3, 4, 5, 6, 10, 12 bottom, 13, 15, 16 right, 17, 18, 21, 25 top, 30 top, 32, 34, 35, 36, 37, 39, 41, 44, 46 bottom, 47, 48 bottom, 50, 51, 53, 56, 60 bottom, 64 top, 65, 66, 67 left, 68, 69, 73, 76, 78, 80 top, 81, 82, 83 top, 88, 91, 92, 94, 96, 97, 99, 101, 104, 106, 108, 128 top, 130, 135 top, 136 bottom)
Reyrolle Parsons & Co. Ltd. (67 right).
Rochdale Equitable Pioneers (52)
Rolls Royce (1971) Ltd. (93 bottom, 127 top)
Science Museum (9, 10 top, 11 left, 12 top, 26, 60 top, 61 bottom, 116 bottom)
Sheffield Library (105)
Sports & General (122 right)
Syndication International (124 bottom)
Wellcome Institute of the History of Medicine (134, 135 bottom, 136 top)

CONTENTS

SECTION 1

The Industrial Revolution

This book traces the social and economic history of Great Britain from the beginnings of what we call the Industrial Revolution to the mid-70s.

The word 'revolution' is often used in history books to describe a violent attempt to overthrow one form of government and replace it by another. The term 'revolution' can also be used, in an engineering sense, to describe one turn of a wheel. In both senses of the word there is movement involved. An industrial revolution therefore means a change in industry, in the manufacture of the requirements of the human race, and these changes have far-reaching social effects.

This first section traces the main changes involved in the Industrial Revolution. It shows the state of Britain at the beginning of the eighteenth century, the size of its towns and its population. Then it goes on to outline the changes in the manufacture of cloth, iron, the development of power-driven machinery and the changes in agriculture needed to feed a growing population, an increasing number of whom were employed in the new processes of manufacturing. It also points out the way in which civil engineers, some of them self-taught men, developed our roads and canal communications in order to cope with the increasing volume of goods and passenger traffic resulting from the industrial and agricultural changes of the period.

1 BRITAIN IN 1700

If one wants to know how many people live in Britain today the answer can easily be found by studying the population figures which have been recorded every ten years. This assessment, or census, has been regularly compiled since the year 1801, the only exception being the period of the Second World War. The census also tells us how people earn their living and thus answers two very important questions concerning (a) the size of the population and (b) its occupations.

How can one find out answers to these questions in a period which did not have census returns? Fortunately there are ways which can provide enough information for an accurate estimate to be made. Tax returns, and parish registers record-in births and deaths can give a guide, and in fact in 1696 a treasury official called Gregory King produced a set of calculations based on returns of the hearth tax which set the population of England and Wales at 5 500 520 (five million, five hundred thousand, five hundred and twenty). The diagram shows King's figures in detail. As you can see King worked out the number of people in each class of society according to rank, and added up the figures for his overall total. For Britain it would probably be safe to assume a population figure of about 6 500 000 (six and a half million).

Most of them lived in the countryside. By our standards there was only one city of any size, and that was London. It had about 650 000 people living in it. It seems very large indeed by the standards of the time, yet regarded as a percentage it probably compares closely with the present day figures, for out of a total population for Britain of about 50 000 000 (fifty million) people, some 8 000 000 (eight million) today live in London. The real difference in population distribution lies in the fact that at the present time there are one million people living in Birmingham, and about three quarters of a million people in Manchester and Liverpool. In 1700 however, Manchester was a large village with about 8 000 people living in it. Salmon were caught in the nearby river Mersey. Its cathedral, it is true, dates back to the fourteenth century, but, even so, the sprawling city of today was then very much a thing of the future. Birmingham was

Family income (p.a.)	Total No. of Persons	No. of Families	Percentage of Total No. of Persons.	Percentage of Total Families.	Occupations etc.,
Over £200	209 520	23 586	4	2	Peers, baronets etc., greater office holders; eminent merchants etc.
£70– £199	440 000	65 000	8	5	Lesser office holders, merchants; clergy; lawyers; Navy officers; greater free-holders.
£38– £69	2 026 000	412 000	37	30	Artisans, tradesmen; lesser clergy; farmers, lesser freeholders etc.,
£14– £37	1 495 000	449 000	27	30	Labouring people and out-servants; soldiers and seamen.
Under £14	1 330 000	400 000	24	30	Cottagers, paupers, vagrants etc.,
TOTALS	5 500 520	1 349 586	100	100	

larger, nearly 25 000 people lived there, but its rapid expansion was still to come. The next largest town to London in 1700 was probably Edinburgh, followed by Bristol, a port growing on the proceeds of slave trading but which was soon to be out-paced by Liverpool, also growing fat on the same trade.

The maps show another important difference in population distribution. In 1700 three fifths of the population of England and Wales lived south of a line stretching from the Bristol Channel to the Wash. The concentration of population associated today with the areas of Lancashire, the West Riding of Yorkshire, the Midlands and the North East of England is missing. The explanation of this lack of population helps to answer the second important question, that of how people earned their living.

The majority of the British people made a living from the land. In many cases they were carrying out what is called subsistence farming (see Chapter 4), in that what they produced was largely eaten by themselves. Some farmers did produce more than they wanted, and they sold this surplus produce. Men with money to spare sometimes put it into

farming in order to make a profit from the sale of surplus produce, but this type of capitalist farmer was in a minority when compared to those whose only aim was to grow their daily bread. Some farmers managed to add to their livelihood by producing cloth on a hand loom in their own home. Perhaps at first they only made cloth for their own family, but an increasing number of these men found it more and more profitable to produce cloth for sale. Indeed in areas of poor quality soil, particularly in Lancashire and the moorland regions of northern and western Britain, it became more profitable to concentrate on the weaving of cloth. For those whose main interests remained in farming, southern England offered a better chance of making a living, than did the hard hills of the Pennines. The basic reason for the fact that more people lived in the southern region of the British Isles rather than the North, was because there was nothing to attract them northwards. Better farming land, easier means of communication, and proximity to the Continent of Europe helped to keep the population concentrated in the south.

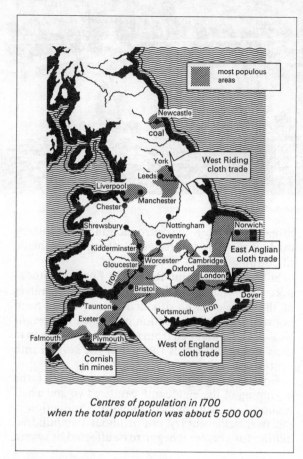

Centres of population in 1700
when the total population was about 5 500 000

Centres of population at the present day
with a total population of about 51 000 000

Industrial Britain at the Beginning of the Eighteenth Century

Despite the importance of agriculture, Britain was an important industrial nation by the beginning of the eighteenth century. Of course the size and scope of present day industry was missing. There were no huge factories, no gleaming lines of cars rolling off the assembly belt. But Britain in 1700 did have a remarkable range of small industries, some of which were to expand rapidly as the century progressed.

Easily the most important was the ancient and internationally famous industry of cloth weaving. There were three main areas which particularly specialized in the making of woollen cloth—that is in addition to those farmers all over the country who supplemented their farming by producing cloth.

These areas were East Anglia, the West Country and the West Riding of Yorkshire. The next chapter describes the way in which the cloth was made and sold. The product was famous, the quality was good, and the men who organized the production and the sale of the cloth saw little need for change in their methods.

The infant cotton industry was struggling to compete with wool at the beginning of the eighteenth century, and so, by contrast, it welcomed change. As cotton became more popular, so

Early eighteenth century Liverpool. A small but growing port with one dock built in 1715.

machinery to speed the processes of its manufacture appeared in the industry. The manufacture of cotton appealed to Lancashire weavers in particular, as they had found it difficult to produce a woollen cloth which could compete in quality with the product of the older established wool manufacturing areas. At the beginning of the seventeenth century it was written about the villagers of Manchester that ... 'they buy cotton wool in London that comes first from Cyprus and Smyrna, and at home work the same ... and then return it to London where the same is vented and sold, and not seldom sent into foreign parts ...' At first, it is true, the Lancashire weavers preferred to mix linen and cotton in order to produce a strong

thread, but later the introduction of machinery made it possible to produce a strong thread made of cotton alone.

Silk was also manufactured in England. Stockport and Macclesfield in Cheshire were centres of this type of cloth production, and it had been boosted by the immigration of French Protestant weavers who had fled from religious persecution in their country towards the end of the seventeenth century.

Coal mining was already important. At the beginning of the eighteenth century two and a half million tons were mined annually. Production in the twentieth century ran at about two hundred million tons before it began to be affected by severe

A coal mine, late eighteenth century. Note the methods of transporting the coal and the steam engine for pumping out water.

Processes involved in the production of iron at the beginning of the nineteenth century.

competition from oil. As the demand for coal increased mines became deeper, and so problems of flooding and ventilating had to be tackled as the eighteenth century progressed. The Northumberland and Durham coalfield had supplied London for hundreds of years by means of the sturdy boats called 'colliers'. Hence coal in London was usually given the name 'sea coal'.

The basic commodity of iron was produced in a variety of places such as South Wales, Sussex, and the Forest of Dean. At the beginning of our period the iron masters were struggling to overcome the drawback of having to depend on charcoal for smelting iron ore (see Chapter 4). The attempts of 'Dud' Dudley, for instance, to use coal instead of wood had failed miserably. The industry badly needed to overcome this drawback, and in fact the use of coal was developed successfully early in the eighteenth century.

The need for more iron was particularly strong in the manufacturing areas such as Birmingham. Brassware, buttons, buckles, nails, pots and pans,

and firearms were produced in a number of small workshops. These small concerns were the forerunners of the massive developments in iron, coal and machinery which were to earn the region the name of the 'Black Country'. Sheffield steel had been mentioned in Chaucer's *Canterbury Tales* in the fourteenth century. The master cutlers of Sheffield needed increased supplies of better quality steel, and again improvement in the processes of manufacture met this need from about 1740.

Apart from these industries there were many other small but vital manufactures at the time, such as glass work, pottery, brewing, leather making, furniture and paper making, all of them important, but which are taken for granted today.

A great obstacle to the future growth of industry and to the rapid movement of goods lay in the development of communications. It is probably true that there have always been grumbles about transport. In our own day they range from the train that is late, to an increase in the fee for a car licence,

5

Interior of a smelting house at Broseley, Shropshire circa 1790.

but the Englishman of the early eighteenth century really did face problems. The only good roads ever constructed in Britain were those built by the Romans about fifteen centuries earlier. These had decayed, but that were often accessible over much of their original routes. Other trackways, often produced by simply using the least inconvenient route from one point to another, were even less satisfactory. Dust in summer, mud in winter and potholes all the year round were the lot of the traveller. A cart often faced the possibility of either breaking its wheels in a deep rut, or breaking its wheels on the stone which had been used to fill up the rut. The depth of these holes led to a crop of stories about travellers finding a hat supposedly floating on a sea of mud, and on bending down to pick it up being told forcibly that the wearer was underneath the hat and on horseback as well!

Water offered a better chance of moving both bulk cargoes and passengers. The collier trade between Newcastle and London has already been mentioned as an example of this, but normal hazards had to be faced in the use of sea transport. Nevertheless much use was made of coastal shipping and navigable rivers, although rivers did not always run obediently to course. The silting up of

An old English waggon. Note the size and shape of the wheels which were a great help in coping with eighteenth century road conditions.

the estuary of the river Dee and its effect on the ancient port of Chester show the difficulties which had to be faced. The Chester merchants made repeated attempts to build new harbours nearer the mouth of the Dee, and in the eighteenth century they carried out a disastrous canalization project which completed the ruin of the port. Only a few kilometres away, however, lay the small but growing port of Liverpool, whose growth was to be closely bound up with the dramatic changes in the industrial face of Britain which commenced in the eighteenth century.

Transferring mails from a mail coach stuck in the snow to a post-chaise.

QUESTIONS

1. Pick out four important towns or cities of the present day and show how they differed in size and importance at the beginning of the eighteenth century.
2. a) Describe the system of cloth manufacture at the beginning of the eighteenth century. Mention the main areas of production and the organization of the industry.
   b) Make a list of other industries that are important today and show how they were organized at the beginning of the eighteenth century.
3. Why was there a problem of communication at the beginning of the eighteenth century? Why would this need to be overcome?

2 THE REVOLUTION IN TEXTILES

The changes in the eighteenth and early nineteenth centuries which are called the Industrial Revolution first appeared in the manufacture of cloth.

Clothing is a basic need of the human race and the importance of the English woollen industry has already been mentioned. Centred on East Anglia, the West of England and the West Riding of Yorkshire it was largely in the hands of individual families. The wool was combed out or carded by the children in the family, spun into a thread by their mother and woven into cloth by their father, all hand-worked processes. As yet the textile mills lay in the future. Daniel Defoe, the author of *Robinson Crusoe*, saw some of these people at work in his travels around England. Near Halifax he came across a 'house-full of lusty fellows, some at the dye-vat ... some in the loom ... all hard at work'. In other cottages Defoe saw children carding and spinning 'hardly anything above four years old but its hands are sufficient to itself'.

These men bought their wool at market, made it up into cloth and then sold it again. Often they bought their wool and then sold back their finished cloth to the same person, known as a clothier. However, in the West of England area of wool production changes in the organization of the textile industries were already beginning to appear. These changes act as a link between the home based

Cottage industry before the machine age.

industry, sometimes called domestic or cottage (see glossary) because of its home centre, and the factory system which was to replace it. A major factor in the change was that the majority of the people carrying out cloth manufacture in the south-west worked for clothiers. Some of these clothiers began to gather the spinners and weavers into one place for the convenience of supplying the wool and collecting the finished cloth. The large sheds put up for this purpose mark one of the beginnings of a factory system.

At the beginning of the eighteenth century, wool was easily the most important industry in all Britain. Well organized with its standards of workmanship controlled by laws drawn up by guilds of cloth manufacturers, its standing in the country was shown by the names connected with it which have remained in everyday use: such as Worsted, the Norfolk village which made a fine quality cloth, and Witney in the South West, a name which has become associated with blankets. The industry was not worried about the possibility of change. It was prosperous, and people wanted its products. They always had wanted them and presumably they always would.

Nevertheless there was a challenge to the supremacy of wool. It has already been pointed out that as early as the end of the sixteenth century, Manchester was experimenting with cotton, the eastern cloth which took its name from the qutan or cotton plant. Lancashire weavers of course had used wool, yet their products had never gained the same stamp of quality as the cloth from the other main centres. Yet Lancashire men needed the extra income from weaving. The poor soils of the county made it vital for many small farmers to have another source of income. The poorer quality of Lancashire woollen cloth actually made it easier for the Lancashire weavers to experiment with cotton because they were not considered important enough to be included within the strict guild control of the woollen industry. And there was a market for cotton. The fashion for lighter clothing which followed the Restoration of Charles II in 1660, created a demand which could only at first be met by silk and linen—expensive and beyond the reach of a modest pocket. Cotton however could meet the same need, and at a much cheaper price. At first calicoes (cotton cloth from Calicut) and chintzes were imported by the East India Company. They became so popular that the woollen manufacturers managed to get Parliament to ban their import. But nothing was said about Lancashire cotton cloth! So Lancashire weavers were able to develop their product thanks to the

protection secured by the woollen manufacturers.

Other factors helped them. The damp mild climate west of the Pennines helped in the spinning of cotton thread. The ports of Liverpool, Preston and Lancaster could import the raw cotton, and when machines appeared in the industry, fast-moving Pennine streams could provide the necessary power. So cotton became the industry associated with Lancashire.

The Machine Revolution

It was also to become the industry first associated with the changes we call the industrial revolution (see glossary). We must first be clear why these changes began to take place in the eighteenth century. The root cause was that demand for cloth was rising rapidly because the population of the country was rising rapidly. It nearly doubled between 1701 and 1801. It was not only our population that increased but also that of Europe, where there was an established market for British cloth. There was also a growing overseas empire to be catered for. The seamen and the merchants of Great Britain were perfectly capable of seeing to it that the goods were delivered to these places.

Any expansion in the production of cloth needed money to finance development and in eighteenth century Britain there were plenty of people, (for instance lawyers, merchants, land owners, shop keepers) who saw in the expanding textile industry a profitable investment for surplus cash. It was inevitable that existing methods of cloth manufacture would prove unequal to meet the rising demand. Hand work gradually gave way to machine power.

These are only the general reasons why machine production replaced hand work. The particular reasons that account for cotton being the first of the textile industries to undergo such a change are to be found in the ease with which the fibre of cotton can be worked by machines, in its cheapness, and in the fact that Lancashire cotton weavers had no guild control hampering their inventiveness.

The Machines

As early as 1598 a university graduate called William Lee had invented the stocking frame which was to herald machine knitting of hosiery. Lee, like later inventors, had to flee from the anger of workmen who thought that their livelihood would vanish. He went to France and finally died, almost forgotten, in Paris.

Machines had also appeared in the silk industry. They appear to have been developed first in Italy. In 1716 an Englishman, Thomas Lombe, went to Leghorn and managed to get drawings of them, then returning triumphant to England. The machines were constructed from his drawings and put into production near Derby. Lombe died not long after this. It was rumoured that a beautiful Italian woman had followed him to England and poisoned him. In any case the high price of raw silk made it difficult for the silk industry to develop in the same manner as Lancashire cotton.

The first stage in the development of cotton machinery was in fact only an improvement in the hand loom. John Kay the man responsible for it was born near Bury. He became known for a small but useful improvement, that of a steel comb instead of one made from wood. Soon after this he turned his attention to another aspect of weaving. On a handloom a weaver passed the cross thread, the weft, in and out of the down threads, the warp. The weaver raised alternate warp threads so that the weft could be passed in and out of the warp. If a cloth wider than the width of a man's reach was being woven, two men had to operate the loom, one passing the weft thread to the other who then returned it. The weft thread passed to and fro on a shuttle. Kay's idea was to send the shuttle and thread along a wooden guide so arranged as not to interfere with the warp. He had two hammers on rods connected to one handle. By working this handle the hammers struck the shuttle from one side of the loom to the other. The whole process only required one hand, leaving the other hand free for combing, and also providing a variable cloth width. But this was only really an improvement, a gadget rather than a revolutionary step forward.

Poor Kay's reward was to see his invention first wrecked and then copied without any money coming to him. After a particularly violent riot his own home in Bury was wrecked. Like Lee years before him, he fled to France.

Here is an extract from the description of the patent—26th May 1733.

'A new invented shuttle for the better and more exact weaving of broadcloths, broad boys, sail cloths or any other broad goods, . . . the weaver sitting in the middle of the loom with great ease and expedition by a small pull at the cord casts or moves the said new invented shuttle from side to side . . .'

As the flying shuttle came into general use the cry was for more cotton yarn. Kay's machine doubled the output of the handlooms. Weavers tramped from one spinner to another looking for thread and once again men with an inventive turn of mind rose to the demand.

Hargreaves' Spinning Jenny.

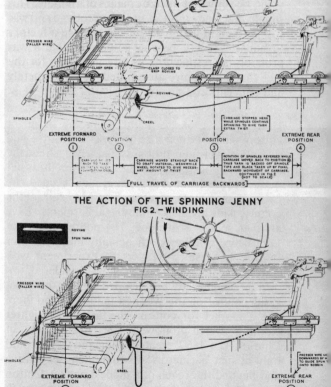

THE ACTION OF THE SPINNING JENNY
FIG I.—DRAFTING AND TWISTING

THE ACTION OF THE SPINNING JENNY
FIG 2.—WINDING

9

Two such men, Lewis Paul and John Wyatt produced a machine which passed raw cotton through pairs of revolving rollers. By turning these rollers at different speeds the thread could be pulled out until a very fine quality was achieved. This thread was then spun off on to spindles which also turned giving a twist to the thread.

Their invention never became generally known. A small factory started by them was never a commercial success and was finally bought up by a certain Richard Arkwright. Yet two of the most important spinning machines that helped to revolutionize the cotton industry contained ideas to be found in Wyatt and Paul's invention.

The first was the 'Spinning Jenny' invented by James Hargreaves in 1763. Hargreaves was a carpenter as well as a weaver, so he was quite able to construct a machine. The 'Jenny', so called either after his wife or simply being a shortened form of 'engine', had a row of eight vertical spindles on to which the thread was wound. All eight spindles could be turned at once by means of a handle. This simple machine could be used in a cottage and was still worked by hand. It did not require a factory to house it and, it became so popular that it was probably as responsible as any invention for the fact that Lancashire abandoned wool completely and concentrated on cotton.

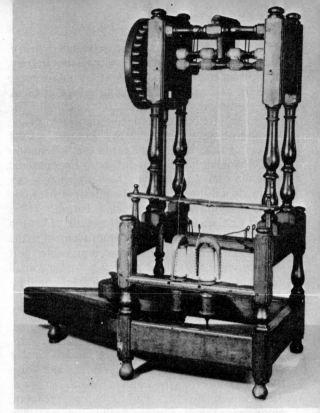

Arkwright's Waterframe in which the thread was stretched as it passed through the rollers at the top.

Sir Richard Arkwright – the successful businessman.

Hargreaves himself did not make a fortune out of his invention, although he did not die in poverty as Kay did. The only real story of success in this list of inventors belongs to Richard Arkwright the inventor of the 'Water Frame', the second of the spinning machines using ideas first tried out by Wyatt and Paul. It was the same Richard Arkwright who had taken over the little factory of Wyatt and Paul. It was also Richard Arkwright who almost certainly took over the idea of a cotton spinning machine worked out by a poor mechanic called Thomas Highs.

Arkwright was a travelling barber and wig maker. In fact he had no training in either carpentry or mechanics. He had never been a weaver, but on his rounds he constantly heard the topic of the need for spinning cotton by a machine, so as to keep pace with the weavers' needs. In 1769 his 'water frame' appeared, four sets of rollers spinning out the thread because of their different speeds and twisting it on to vertical spindles. The big difference between this and the earlier inventions was that it required water power to operate it. This meant that the machine had to be housed near to fast moving streams, in buildings specially designed for it. The move to factory work from cottage work was bound to develop rapidly. Ark-

A replica of Crompton's Mule – the carriage in the foreground moved along the rail and so stretched the thread.

Samuel Crompton – the unsuccessful businessman.

wright's first factory was situated at Cromford near Derby, where the river Derwent gave him his source of power. It was this use of water power that led to the term 'mill' being applied to the new textile factories. It still is.

Was Arkwright the Inventor?

To try to piece the story together is almost like reading a detective novel. *Twenty years* after Arkwright produced his model, Thomas Highs claimed that he had thought of it first. He quoted a conversation with Arkwright. Highs claimed that Arkwright said to him one evening in a public house that spinning (cotton) by rollers 'will never be brought to bear'. Highs replied 'I think that I could bring that to bear'. Then, according to Highs, Arkwright asked him to make a model. Highs did so and soon after this Arkwright's machine appeared! The only real factor in Arkwright's favour is the long gap of nearly twenty years which elapsed between Arkwright's machine and Highs' claim. This can however be accounted for by the fact that Arkwright was a born man of business if no inventor. Highs, an inventor, was no man of business and had no idea how to cash in on his ideas.

Whatever the rights and wrongs of the matter, the Lancashire cotton industry now had a machine, the 'Jenny' producing a strong weft thread, and the water frame giving a strong warp thread. It was due to the brilliance of Samuel Crompton that his 'Mule' turned out a fine thread capable of being used for either warp of weft yet fine enough for muslin. It combined the type of rollers used on the water frame and the moving carriage idea of the jenny. Poor Crompton made little from his in-

vention. Even while working on it in his fine Elizabethan style house, which can still be seen at Bolton, he was spied on, people peering in at his windows from ladders. Finally knowing that he could not keep his secret indefinitely he offered his machine to the local manufacturers. They in return promised him a subscription. It raised £67.32½. This from men who made their fortunes from his invention. Many years later Parliament granted him £5000 but it only paid his heavy debts. Crompton like Kay, Highs and Hargreaves, did not possess the business sense of a Richard Arkwright.

If we pause for a moment and list the inventions described so far, it becomes obvious that the balance between spinning and weaving was again badly adjusted. The improvement in weaving brought about by Kay had put spinning at a disadvantage, but then came three spinning machines, those of Hargreaves, Arkwright and Highs, and Crompton.

To restore the balance weaving needed machinery. It came in the form of the power loom of Edmund Cartwright. Cartwright's background was very different to that of the mechanic, the carpenter and the barber. Educated at Oxford he became a clergyman and it was only because of a holiday at Matlock, near Arkwright's mills, that he found out about the cotton industry and its need for a power loom. Cartwright tackled the problem and produced a machine which threw the shuttles by springs. This, with later improvements and with the use of steam power, became the basis of his machine. Like Crompton he almost ruined himself in his effort to work his own machines in factories. One was burned to the ground, possibly through the actions of hostile hand loom weavers.

11

Power loom weaving.

In the end Cartwright got a grant of £10 000 from Parliament which left him enough to buy a farm in Kent.

Both the spinning and the weaving of cotton could now be done by machinery, but the change was gradual. The first power loom did not appear in Manchester until 1806. Handloom weavers were still eking out a living in the 1830's and 1840's (See Chapter 9). The important point is that the means of mechanization existed by the beginning of the nineteenth century.

The same type of change inevitably appeared in the older woollen industry. Arkwright's water frame was in action by 1786 in Yorkshire. Boulton and Watt were putting up two large engines in 1789 in the Leeds area. Much woollen spinning was done on Crompton's mule, which seems to have been very suitable for this operation. It was not until the middle of the nineteenth century however, that wool was machine combed. Nor was power weaving general in the woollen industry until the second half of the nineteenth century.

QUESTIONS

1. Briefly describe how cloth was made and marketed at the beginning of the eighteenth century.
2. What factors caused a rising demand for cloth which helped to lead to the machine revolution?
3. Describe the inventions associated with the names of Kay; Hargreaves; Arkwright and Crompton.

The Soho Manufactory near Birmingham belonging to Boulton and Watt, where the latter developed his steam engine.

3   POWER SOURCES AND FACTORIES

The use of machinery in the production of textiles had many consequences. For instance hand power could no longer drive machines such as Arkwright's water frame and Crompton's mule, and new power sources needed to be developed. The ever increasing production of cloth meant that, in turn, the finishing processes of bleaching and printing, also needed revolutionizing. In addition, the new machinery needed the special, purpose-built buildings we call factories. Finally as the next chapter shows, the development of machines and mechanical power meant an ever-increasing demand for coal and iron which helped to account for equally great changes in those industries.

The traditional finishing processes for cloth were simple. The cloth was stretched out on tenterhooks exposed to the sun's rays and was then treated with potash and finally with sour milk. It was obviously not very satisfactory to depend on the rays of the sun in the British climate, and the whole process could be very drawn out. The answer lay in the use of chemicals, and in providing this answer the foundations of the chemical industry were laid.

From about the middle of the eighteenth century dilute sulphuric acid began to replace sour milk. In 1785 the chemist Berthollet discovered that chlorine would bleach vegetable fibres, and from about 1787 chlorine was being used to bleach cloth in both England and Scotland. As a consequence of rising demand, Charles Tennant set up a factory near Glasgow in 1799 which began to produce chloride of lime as a bleaching powder. The textile industry also began to provide a more elaborate choice of patterns when the printing process was speeded up by T. Bell of Preston, who brought out a system of rollers for cylindrical printing, rather like the way newspapers are printed today.

A more far-reaching and drawn out process was the way in which water and then steam power became the driving forces of the textile industry. Water was an obvious first choice for providing the power to drive machinery, for the waterwheel had been known to man for many centuries. Arkwright and the other early mill owners looked for fast-running streams when they considered where their factories were to be sited, and for a time the Lancashire cotton industry spread out into neighbouring counties such as Derbyshire and Nottinghamshire looking for suitable river valleys. Steam power however made all this unnecessary. The coal needed for the provision of steam power could be obtained in Lancashire itself, and the Lancashire cotton mill of today has kept its name only as a reminder of its one time dependence on water.

Calico printing.

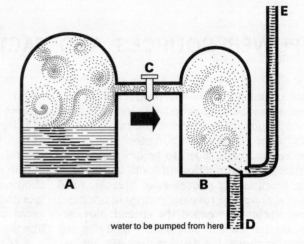

1. Steam from boiler A passed into tank B

2. Tap C was then closed and cold water was poured on to the sides of the tank B, the steam condensed leaving a partial vacuum

3. Water rose through pipe D until the tank was nearly full

4. Steam was then readmitted thus driving the water out through pipe E

water to be pumped from here

The principle of Savery's engine

The Steam Engine

Of course steam power did not only develop because of the textile revolution, but it hastened the process of change in two ways, for not only did the steam engine drive the machines, but it also helped to provide the necessary coal by pumping out the mines as they went deeper. In fact it was in connection with mining that the steam engine first found a use. Initially, it was in effect nothing more than a pump. This practical use of steam power had been known to the ancient Greeks, but having no need for it they had not developed it. It was a Cornishman, Thomas Savery, in the seventeenth century, trying to help the tin and copper mining industry of that county, who developed what we should term a steam pump. A model of his machine was shown to William III in 1698, well before the age of machinery in the textile industry. Savery hoped to use it not only to pump out mines, but to supply water to houses and to turn the wheels of flour mills; but as his engine had no safety valve, explosions could and did happen. People turned eagerly to the engine of Thomas Newcomen.

The Newcomen Engine

Newcomen was a blacksmith from Darmouth in Devon, and again we have an example of a skilled workman producing something based on practical experience. He may have heard of Savery, who had worked not far away, but his engine was a separate development. In a way Savery's engine followed a better principle because it made use of the expansion of steam. Newcomen however used steam to create a vacuum through condensation, and atmospheric pressure did the rest. But Newcomen had a safety valve fitted to later models of his engine; Savery's model had not possessed such a refinement, with disastrous results!

As the diagram shows, the Newcomen engine produced a to and fro movement. This in itself, although adequate for the pumping of water, was not suitable for supplying motive power to textile machinery. In addition, even if this obstacle had been overcome, there remained the fact that the constant cooling of the cylinder in order to condense the steam (see diagram) led to a great wastage of heat and also of coal. These problems were to be solved by James Watt.

James Watt

Carpenters, barbers and blacksmiths have appeared in the list of inventors associated with the Industrial Revolution. James Watt was a different type of man. He had received the benefit of education, in that he spoke several languages in addition to his great interest in things mechanical. The University of Glasgow gave him a post as maker of

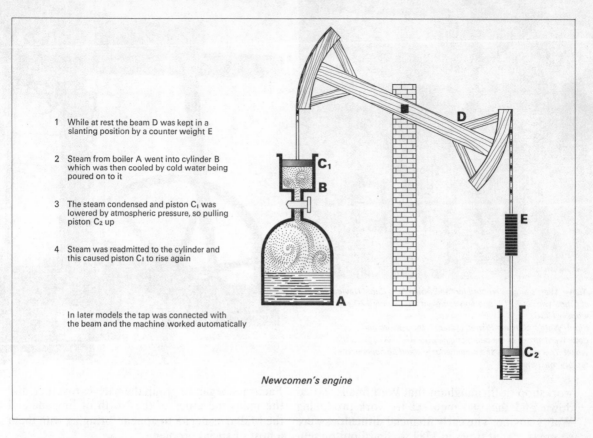

1 While at rest the beam D was kept in a slanting position by a counter weight E

2 Steam from boiler A went into cylinder B which was then cooled by cold water being poured on to it

3 The steam condensed and piston C_1 was lowered by atmospheric pressure, so pulling piston C_2 up

4 Steam was readmitted to the cylinder and this caused piston C_1 to rise again

In later models the tap was connected with the beam and the machine worked automatically

Newcomen's engine

James Watt.

scientific instruments and provided him with his own workshop and it was there, in 1763, that he first received a model of the Newcomen engine. Watt made an examination of it and realized the drawbacks mentioned above. He saw that the answer to the loss of power lay in ensuring that condensation was complete, and also that steam pressure should be used to work the pistons.

As Watt said, 'To avoid useless condensation the vessel in which the steam acted upon the piston aught always to be as hot as the steam itself . . . the steam must be condensed in a separate vessel'. Thus came the idea of the separate condenser. Watt developed his engine and, most important, adopted the 'sun and planet' idea of William Murdoch, his inventive foreman at the Birmingham Soho Works where the engines were made. This meant that his steam engine developed a rotary movement suitable for driving machinery. Thus both the drawbacks of the Newcomen engine had been overcome.

Watt went into partnership with two men in order to make and sell his engines. His first partnership with Roebuck, of the Carron Iron Works in Scotland, was not a success. His second, with Matthew Boulton, was. It was at Boulton's Soho

Above, Watt's engine erected for the Birmingham Canal Navigation at Smethwick in 1777, and only removed after nearly 120 years work in 1898.
Right, Watt's 'Sun and Planet' system – the upward and downward stroke of the beam engine operated the cogs on the wheel. This meant that the steam engine could be applied to factory machinery.

workshop in Birmingham that Watt finally settled down and the two men set to work producing Watt's engine. The early financial difficulties were so great that at times in 1781 we find Boulton selling property and unable to pay wages, and it was not until 1786 that the firm had cleared off their debts. Yet an engine of theirs had been in use in France as early as 1779, in addition to some British sales. Once the firm was really on its feet its faith in. the Watts' engine was shown by their terms. Anyone buying their engine paid for the costs of setting it up and then paid the firm *one third* of the difference in the running costs between a Newcomen engine and the Watt model.

From about 1785 orders for the Boulton & Watt steam engine flowed in from the cotton spinners. In 1787 Robert Peel, grandfather of the prime minister, ordered it. Richard Arkwright had installed them in 1790 and in the 1790's they began to appear in the woollen industry. From the early years of the nineteenth century they began to be used to drive the new power looms. They were also used for milling flour, in flint mills and for crushing sugar cane.

Steam power freed the builders of factories from the need to search for water power first. The only point that needed to be considered was the availability of coal. This was plentiful, for new means of communications were making it easier to move coal from mines to the place where it was needed.

Factories began to group themselves together, and the industrial cities of the North of England and the Midlands began to appear, bringing with them a host of social problems.

Other Industries

Although the most spectacular changes took place in textiles, other industries showed the same tendency at this time to become machine powered.

A good example is to be found in printing. The growing population, despite the lack of compulsory education, needed more books and newspapers as well as more clothing. A German, Frederick Koenig, came to England in 1806 and invented a steam driven hand press with automatic inked rollers. This was used by *The Times* for the first time on November 29, 1814. A paper making machine had already appeared a few years earlier.

Another important industry undergoing a revolutionary change at this time was that of pottery. In 1700 the term 'pottery making' implied a cottage with an oven outside, surrounded by sods to conserve the heat. It was rather like the cottage system of cloth production in that the clay was prepared by the children and the 'throwing' and finishing was carried out by the father. In Staffordshire the potters used an inferior yellow type of clay which they coated with white clay.

The road to the large scale industrial development of pottery lay in the use of coal and by importing kaolin (china clay) from Devon and Cornwall. The most important factor, however, was one person, Josiah Wedgewood. His works near Burslem, known as 'Etruria', employed hundreds of work people and is the equivalent in pottery of Arkwright's cotton mill.

QUESTIONS

1. a) What processes were introduced into the preparation of cloth in the eighteenth century?
   b) Explain why some factories are called 'mills'.
2. Copy out the diagram of Newcomen and Watt's engine. Explain how James Watt improved on the Newcomen design.
3. What consequences followed from the development of steam power?

4   IRON AND COAL

The Iron Industry

At the beginning of the eighteenth century manufacturers of iron goods in Britain were running short of home-produced iron, and pig iron was being imported in increasing quantities from Sweden and Russia. The difficulty facing British iron producers was a serious shortage of timber in the traditional iron smelting regions, such as the Weald in Sussex and the Forest of Dean in Gloucestershire, where the timber was used to make charcoal to fuel the smelting furnaces. To overcome this difficulty some iron masters moved to new areas such as Shropshire, North and South Wales, Cumberland and even the Highlands of Scotland, where timber and fast-flowing streams to power the forge hammers and furnace bellows were available. Other iron producers, as we shall see, turned to coal as a possible substitute for charcoal.

Coalbrookdale, Shropshire, where in 1709 good quality pig iron was produced by smelting iron ore with coke instead of charcoal.

Abraham Darby

Coal was available in this country in enormous quantities, but it had never been successfully used to smelt iron ore because the impurities in coal, especially suphur, made the iron produced in coal furnaces too brittle. In 1709, however, Abraham Darby, an iron master who had moved to Coalbrookdale in Shropshire to make use of the local timber supplies, succeeded in producing good quality iron in a furnace burning coke as fuel. Darby's success was partly good luck. The local Shropshire 'clod coal', from which he made his coke, was particularly suitable for smelting, but even so, his coke smelting process was an important milestone in the progress of the iron industry. The method was later improved by his son and grandson, and Darby's Coalbrookdale works (which is shown in the previous picture with some of its products in the foreground) deserves an honoured place in the story of the development of modern industry.

'Iron Mad' Wilkinson

In the second half of the eighteenth century there was a greatly increased demand for iron. A series of wars against France for which arms were needed, the use of new machines in the textile trade and other industries described in earlier chapters, and the demand for iron goods from the growing population, all had the effect of encouraging the spread of Darby's ideas and the expansion of the iron industry. As a result, iron manufacture began

to move from the isolated woodland regions in which it was carried out before 1750 to the coalfields, and several famous ironworks were set up by a number of individual iron masters of whom the best known is probably 'Iron Mad' Wilkinson.

Wilkinson, who was born in 1728, was one of the first industrial 'tycoons' with interests in a number of ironworks in Britain and France, and shares in mining companies in Wales and Cornwall. Like Dr. John Roebuck, who set up the Carron Iron Works in Scotland in 1759, Wilkinson saw that there was a big future in iron at the time of the

John Wilkinson's iron works in the west midlands

The first iron bridge ever constructed. It was made at the Darby Works, Coalbrookdale and stands crossing the river Severn near Broseley. The arch is circular with a span of 30 metres and a rise of 12 metres. The bridge is preserved as an industrial monument.

Seven Years War (1756–1763) when the demand for armaments was at its height, and in the last year of the war he built an ironworks at Broseley in the South Staffordshire coalfield. This ironworks was a success and Wilkinson set up several others in the West Midlands and North Wales in the years which followed. In them he pioneered a number of new techniques and new uses for iron which earned for him the title 'Iron Mad'.

Wilkinson improved the technique of casting iron and supplied James Watt with the accurate parts which made his early steam engines so efficient. He developed a boring machine to make cannon barrels which also helped Watt, by providing him with accurate cylinders for the steam engines he produced at Boulton's Soho works in Birmingham. In his turn Wilkinson bought steam engines from the Soho factory to blow the blast at his iron furnaces, probably the first iron master to do so. In addition he designed and manufactured iron chairs, iron pipes for drainage and water supply and iron brewers vats. He worked with the third Abraham Darby to produce the world's first iron bridge which was erected across the River Severn in 1779. In 1787 he floated the first ever iron barge on the same river, to the amazement of a large crowd which had gathered to watch it sink. Finally, when he died in 1805, 'Iron Mad' Wilkinson was buried in an iron coffin beneath an iron tomb, a fitting end for the man who is often called 'the father of the iron trade'.

Cort's Puddling Process

Wilkinson's work was with cast iron, and it was this material smelted with coke fuel which was produced at the many ironworks which sprang up on the coalfields of this country after 1750. Cast iron has certain drawbacks however. It is brittle and cannot be worked as wrought iron can. For some purposes, for example the moving parts in machinery, it is quite unsuitable because it will not stand up to constant strain. Not surprisingly, therefore, iron manufacturers in the late eighteenth century were looking for a method of making wrought iron which was quicker and easier than the traditional method of heating pig iron in charcoal, and then laboriously hammering out the carbon and other impurities.

The answer to this problem was provided by Henry Cort, the owner of a small ironworks at Fontley in Hampshire. In 1783 and 1784 Cort took out patents for a method of making wrought iron in a reverberatory furnace like the one illustrated

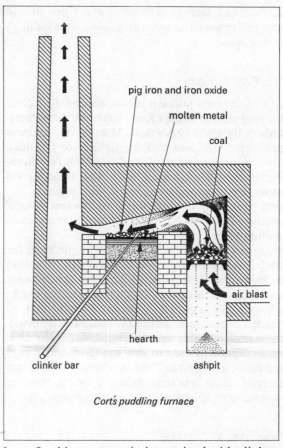

Cort's puddling furnace

here. In this process pig iron mixed with clinkers rich in iron oxide was placed in the furnace and heated with coal, care being taken to keep the fuel separate from the iron. When the iron was in a semi-molten state it was stirred or 'puddled' with a long rod called a clinker bar, which encouraged the iron oxide to unite with the carbon in the pig iron and be driven off as carbon dioxide gas. The resulting iron, now free of its carbon, was removed from the furnace and forced through rollers which pressed out any remaining impurities. Thus it emerged as good quality wrought iron, made in a fraction of the time taken by the traditional method.

Cort, like many other eighteenth century inventors, received little financial return from his work, but his puddling and rolling process was of the utmost importance. It was adopted by Richard Crawshay at his Cyfarthfa Ironworks at Merthyr Tydfil in 1787 and was improved by Homfray at the nearby Pen-y-daren Ironworks soon after, thus turning South Wales into the world's leading producer of wrought iron, and Merthyr Tydfil into a great industrial centre. By the end of the eighteenth century therefore, as a result of the work

19

of men like Darby, Wilkinson and Cort, Britain had the largest and most up to date iron industry in Europe.

The Coal Industry

In 1700 coal was mined in all the major British coal-bearing regions except Kent, but by modern standards output was very small. Most of the coal was mined for local use in domestic fires or for small scale domestic industry, and only the Northumberland and Durham coalfield, which had a good outlet for its produce via the River Tyne, had any real economic importance. The amount of coal produced in 1700 has been estimated at about $2\frac{1}{2}$ million tons.

During the eighteenth century the demand for coal increased very considerably. The new iron industry, the steam engines which were beginning to power the textile mills, the engineering works which began to grow in areas like Birmingham, all needed coal as fuel, and so the coal industry began to change in order to satisfy their needs. By 1800 coal output had risen to 10 million tons and in 1815 the figure had risen to 27 million tons. This increase in production was made possible by the removal of a number of obstacles to mining progress.

Obstacles to Progress

Flooding. The need to produce more coal resulted in deeper mining because the deposits of coal near the surface soon became used up. Sinking deep shafts immediately brought the problem of flooding however, as water gathered in the underground galleries quicker than it could be removed by the primitive systems of drainage in use before 1700. The answer to this problem, as we saw in Chapter 3, was the use of steam power. Newcomen's engine was specially designed to pump water out of the deep seams in the Cornish tin mines, and it was not long before beam engines, cast at Darby's Coalbrookdale works, were in use on the South Staffordshire coalfield. From there their use spread to other mining districts, and by 1767 one hundred Newcomen engines were in use on Tyneside alone. Improvements to the pumping engine by James Watt greatly increased its efficiency, as we have seen, and by 1800 the problem of flooding had been overcome.

Ventilation. Deep mining also created problems of ventilation. Without a good supply of fresh air

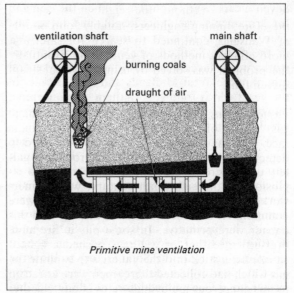

Primitive mine ventilation

miners could not work properly, and poisonous and explosive gases were liable to collect underground. The first answer to this problem was to lower a brazier of burning coals into a second shaft, which drew fresh air through the mine rather in the way an open fire can cause draughts through a room. 'Coursing' systems consisting of wooden partitions caused the air to follow well defined routes and ensured that every gallery had a supply of fresh air. In many pits this method of ventilation was very dangerous. Explosive gas drawn out of the mine frequently ignited when it came into contact with the burning coals, and serious accidents

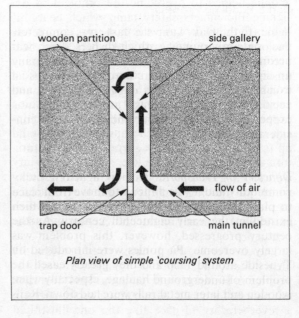

Plan view of simple 'coursing' system

resulted. Throughout the eighteenth century, therefore, mining engineers, notably John Buddle of Wallsend, continued to search for safer and more efficient methods of ventilation. Eventually the problem was solved by using powerful steam driven fans.

Explosive Gas. 'Fire damp' (explosive methane gas) is one of the greatest dangers coal miners face. The gas is lighter than air and very hard to detect, and it can collect under the roof of a gallery until there is sufficient to cause a serious explosion. In the eighteenth century, when miners worked by the light of candles, such accidents were common. At first the methods of dealing with this danger were primitive. In some pits a 'fire man' dressed in leather or wet rags pushed a lighted candle on a stick into the galleries to explode the gas which had collected there; men were attracted to this dangerous job by high rates of pay. In other mines, steel mills were used to give light by giving off a shower of sparks none of which was large enough to ignite the gas. In especially dangerous pits miners even worked in the faint phosphorescent glow given off by rotting fish, but despite all these devices accidents continued.

In the early nineteenth century the public became concerned at the number of pit accidents and at the numbers of miners who lost their lives. Thus in 1815 The Society for the Prevention of Mining Accidents was set up in Sunderland. Sir Humphrey Davy, the most famous scientist of the day, was called in to advise on the question of explosions and he helped to overcome the problem by designing the miners safety lamp which bears his name. In the Davy lamp the flame was completely enclosed in wire gauze which dispersed the heat before it could ignite the gas. Unfortunately many unscrupulous mine owners used the lamps as an excuse to work especially dangerous seams, and accidents did not decrease as sharply as was expected, although output increased very considerably.

Difficulty of Transport. Coal is a heavy, bulky commodity and it was difficult to move from place to place with the poor means of transport which existed in the early eighteenth century. As the century progressed, however, this problem was largely overcome. Pit ponies were introduced on Tyneside around 1750 and they greatly eased the problem of underground haulage, especially when wooden and later metal rails were laid down. Rails

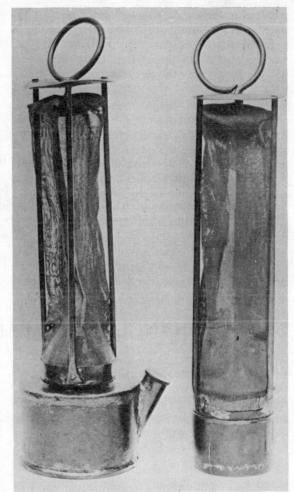

The first Davy lamps.

were also put down on the surface to improve pit head transport and with the development of a national system of canals coal could be moved easily from one part of the country to another. The coming of railways in the early nineteenth century speeded up this process still further, and it is significant that the first canal in this country, built by the Duke of Bridgewater in 1761, and Stephenson's first successful railway, which opened between Stockton and Darlington in 1825, were both built to serve coalmines.

The Importance of Coal

The solutions to the problems outlined above and the development of more efficient winding gear transformed the coal industry. As we shall see in a later chapter, social advances did not always keep

21

pace with technical progress and miners' living and working conditions were frequently disgraceful, but in economic terms the industry had changed out of all recognition. Output rose year by year throughout the nineteenth century, reaching a climax in 1913 when a record 287 million tons of coal was brought to the surface. This abundant supply of home produced coal was the foundation on which the rest of Britain's industrial prosperity was built.

QUESTIONS

1. What contribution did Abraham Darby, 'Iron Mad' Wilkinson and Henry Cort make to the progress of the iron industry?
2. What factors led to an increase in the demand for coal during the eighteenth century?
3. What were the main obstacles in the way of progress in the coal industry in the eighteenth and early nineteenth centuries? How were these obstacles overcome?
4. What importance did coal have in the Industrial Revolution?

5 THE CHANGES IN FARMING

In 1700 Britain was an agricultural country. Only one fifth of the population lived in towns (as against more than four fifths today) and most people worked on the land or were engaged in one of the trades closely associated with farming.

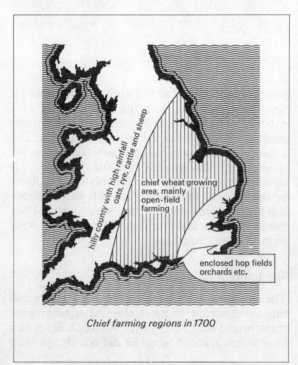

Chief farming regions in 1700

Agriculture in 1700

Over much of the country farming had hardly changed since the middle ages. In the north and west where the land is hilly and where sheep and cattle rearing were more important than crop growing, farms were generally enclosed (see later in this chapter) and consisted of compact fields separated by fences and hedges; but over much of the really fertile arable region of the country further south open-field farming was still carried on. Villages in that area often consisted of three large fields divided into strips, and the simple three year crop rotation, which allowed one field to lie fallow while the other two were planted with grain, was followed. The village animals were grazed on the common land as they had been for generations, and the villagers had their ancient rights of grazing pigs, collecting wood and cutting turf on the waste, the rough marsh, and the scrub and woodland which lay beyond the common pasture. Village life was organized by the Lord of the Manor who, in addition to his holdings in the big fields, usually owned a separate enclosed 'manor' or 'home' farm; names which survive to this day in many English villages.

By modern standards this open-field farming was very inefficient. The strips in the big fields were separated from each other by small walls of earth called balks, and these, together with the pathways which threaded through the fields, wasted an enormous amount of good land. Leaving a field fallow each year to recover its goodness was also very wasteful and meant that only two thirds of the village land was really productive. The absence of hedges and fences allowed weeds to spread easily from one strip to the next and encouraged animals to stray into the growing crops. A further problem arose because the three year rotation did not include root crops or artificial grasses, like clover, which are now used as winter feed for livestock, and as a result most of the village animals were slaughtered in the autumn and the meat salted down. Finally there were problems caused by the joint ownership and use of the common. Few farmers were prepared to spend their own time and money improving land they did not own, and the village pasture land was frequently undrained and of very poor quality. This naturally led to diseases among the livestock and on unfenced common such diseases spread like wildfire. For all these reasons the yield from an open-field village was very low and has been estimated as about half the yield obtainable from an enclosed village of the same size.

Why then did open-field agriculture last for so long? The answer lies chiefly in the very small population of those days. Only 6½ million people lived in England, Scotland and Wales at the beginning of the eighteenth century and even the inefficient farming methods of the time could supply most of their food needs. Only round London,

which even then had a population of nearly 700 000, had it been found necessary to change the methods of arable farming. Kent with its enclosed orchards, market gardens and hop fields was an example of how an increased demand for food could alter the traditional ways of producing it.

The Agricultural Revolution

After 1700 the situation began to change. To begin with there was a rapid increase in population, especially after 1750, and the figure of 6½ million in 1700 had doubled to 13 million by 1815. This meant many more mouths to feed. Throughout the eighteenth century there was a gradual rise in the general standard of living in this country which was reflected in an increasing demand for meat and for wheat flour for white bread. In addition, as we have seen in the previous chapters, the town populations of the manufacturing districts began to grow in the late eighteenth century and since these people no longer grew their own food, the country areas round about had to produce more for them. This was particularly the case after 1793 when the war against France broke out and seriously disrupted food supplies from abroad, making Britain more dependent on her own farms.

The overall effect of these factors was to make farming more profitable than it had ever been before. The demand for home produced food was

An early farm machine for planting seed in neat rows.

four Wheel Drill Plow, with a Seed and a Manure Hopper, was first Invented in the Year 1745 is now in Use with Wᵐ Ellis at Little Gaddesden near Hempstead in Hertfordshire, where any person view the same. It is so light that a Man may Draw it, but Generally drawn by a Pony or little Horse

growing, and with the improvements in transport after 1750 it was possible for farmers to supply more distant markets. It was natural therefore that go-ahead landlords should look round for ways and means of increasing their output, and the result was a number of important changes in farming which, taken together, are often called the Agricultural Revolution.

Farming Pioneers

One aspect of the Agricultural Revolution was the spread of much more scientific farming. New techniques were tried out by a number of enterprising landlords whose success did much to change British agriculture.

1. *Jethro Tull.* One of the first of these was Jethro Tull, who was born at Basildon in Berkshire in 1674. He turned to farming after spending some years as a lawyer. Perhaps it was because he had not been a countryman all his life, that he farmed Mount Prosperous, his Berkshire estate, in a way which aroused both surprise and hostility among his neighbours and his labourers. To improve his land he deep ploughed and regularly hoed it, and he experimented with various new crop rotations to make more intensive use of his fields. He abandoned the traditional method of sowing seed broadcast, and instead planted it in straight rows which could be hoed while the crop was growing. This caused a strike among his field labourers who thought seed ought to be sown as it had been in the Bible, and partly because of this Tull invented in 1701 the seed drill. By doing so Tull brought mechanization to British farming, and he later invented a horse drawn hoe so that the whole process of sowing and weeding could be done by machine. Most of Tull's neighbours regarded him as a crank, but his book *The New Horse Hoeing Husbandry*, published in 1731, had a very important influence later in the century, and Tull deserves to be remembered as one of the first scientific farmers who based his ideas not on tradition, but on experiment and careful observation.

2. *Lord Townshend.* 'Turnip' Townshend was a contemporary of Tull's and like him he only came to farming after years spent following another career. Townshend had been British Ambassador in Holland, Lord Lieutenant of Ireland and a Secretary of State and but for a quarrel with the Prime Minister, Robert Walpol, he might well have

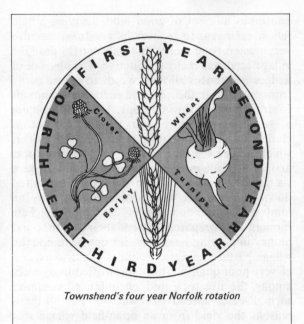

Townshend's four year Norfolk rotation

spent all his life in politics. As it was he retired in 1730 to his estate at Raynham in Norfolk, and spent the last years of his life putting it in order. The estate was badly neglected and consisted of tracts of badly drained sandy soil where it was said that 'two rabbits struggled for every blade of grass', but Townshend enthusiastically overcame all the difficulties. He drained, marled and deep ploughed the land to improve the top soil, and used, instead of the traditional three year rotation, a four year course in which he planted wheat in the first year, turnips in the second, barley in the third and clover in the fourth. The turnips and clover not only enriched his soil but also provided good winter feed for livestock, and Townshend became such an enthusiast for turnips that his constant references to them earned him his famous nickname. In the short time he spent at Raynham between his retirement and his death in 1738, Townshend helped to transform English agriculture. He showed that light soils could produce good crops if they were carefully cultivated and the four year rotation which he did so much to popularize was coming into use all over the eastern counties by the end of the century.

3. *Robert Bakewell.* Robert Bakewell took over the management of his family's farm at Dishley in Leicestershire in 1760. His main concern was to improve the quality of the livestock on the farm and he enthusiastically used root crops for winter feed and insisted on clean stalls and kind treatment

The Durham oxen – their weight was 2472 lbs and 2437 lbs.

for his beasts. His most important contribution however was successfully to develop the technique of carefully controlled selective breeding. He chose animals with characteristics he wanted to encourage, for example beasts which had short legs and heavy shoulders and flanks, and bred only from these. By keeping careful records and cross-breeding the improved stock he gradually built up his famous New Leicestershire breed of sheep, and had some success too with cattle and pigs. These ideas impressed other farmers, and after a visit to Dishley Grange to see Bakewell's flock, Charles and Robert Colling of Ketton, near Darlington, used the same technique to develop the Durham Shorthorn breed of cattle. Soon go-ahead stock-breeders all over the country were using selective breeding to improve their flocks and herds and their success can be judged from the following table of average weights of beasts sold at Smithfield market in London.

	1710	1795
Oxen	370 lbs	800 lbs
Calves	50 lbs	150 lbs
Sheep	38 lbs	80 lbs

4. *Squire Coke*. Thomas Coke of Holkham in Norfolk was probably the most famous farmer of his day, and his enormous success persuaded many other landlords to adopt the new techniques. When Coke took over his estate in 1776 it was worth no more than £2000 a year. When he died as Earl of

Sheep in 1680 and 1808 – the improvement the result of the work of Robert Bakewell.

The Rotherham plough, manufactured at the town in Yorkshire. The original model (not shown here) had two shares, the second fitting above the ordinary share to shield the breast.

Leicester in 1842, it was worth more than £20 000 a year and he had transformed it from a poor, sandy, badly drained property into one of the most up-to-date farms in the country. This was done by the use of better implements like the new Rotherham type plough, the use of the four year rotation, proper drainage and deep ploughing, and the introduction of bone manure and cattle cake. Coke planted carefully-sited trees to act as windbreaks and encouraged his tenants to sink their own money in farm improvements by granting them long leases. Each year at sheep shearing time, when Coke invited hundreds of guests to his home, they could not fail to be impressed by all they saw on his estate. Townshend, Coke and his go-ahead neighbours, like the Duke of Bedford at Woburn, made Norfolk into one of the richest farming counties in the country and a leader in the Agricultural Revolution.

5. *Arthur Young.* Unlike the pioneers we have looked at so far, Arthur Young was not a successful farmer, in fact his attempt to become one had ended in financial failure. He nevertheless deserves a place in any history of farming because of the important influence he had through his writings. Young was the first great farming journalist and in a long series of books, pamphlets and articles which he began writing in 1767, he did much to promote better methods of agriculture. He travelled all over the country visiting up-to-date farms and noting down everything he saw. He persuaded leading farmers, including King George III, who wrote under the pen name of Ralph Robinson, to contribute articles to his farming magazine 'The Annals of Agriculture', and in 1793 when Pitt's government set up the Board of Agriculture, Young was the obvious choice to become its first secretary. He worked hard for the board collecting statistics, offering advice and writing its annual reports right up to his death in 1820. Arthur Young gave publicity to the Agricultural Revolution and this was a very important contribution. He also, incidentally, left a mass of information about the

eighteenth century which is of great value to the present day economic historian.

The Enclosure Movement

The biggest single obstacle to the adoption of the ideas outlined in the previous section was the existence of the open-field villages. With their traditional and rather haphazard methods they put a brake on agricultural progress and the first thing enterprising landlords did when they wanted to try out the new techniques was to enclose their land.

This idea of enclosure was not new. Large areas of the north and west had been enclosed in Tudor times when many landlords had found it profitable to fence off their fields and the common in order to keep sheep, and enclosures had gone on here and there, mostly for cattle farms, throughout the seventeenth century. What was different about the eighteenth century enclosure movement was its scale, (some $2\frac{1}{2}$ million hectares, or nearly one quarter of the total cultivated land, were enclosed) and the fact that most of the enclosures were made in order to improve arable farming. The following table of enclosure acts passed by Parliament is therefore a very good guide to the progress of the farming revolution which began slowly in the first half of the eighteenth century, speeded up after 1750 and reached a climax during the Napoleonic Wars when the demand for home grown wheat was at its height.

Year	Number of Enclosure Acts
1714–20	6
1720–30	33
1730–40	35
1740–50	38
1750–60	156
1760–70	424
1770–80	642
1780–90	287
1790–1800	506
1800–1810	906

The process by which a village was enclosed was fairly straight forward. Sometimes it was done by a simple agreement, sometimes by Act of Parliament. Usually if the owners of four fifths of the village land agreed to it, a petition was sent to Parliament asking for an enclosure act to be passed. Commissioners appointed by Parliament then visited the village and surveyed and valued all the land and checked everyone's legal claim to a share.

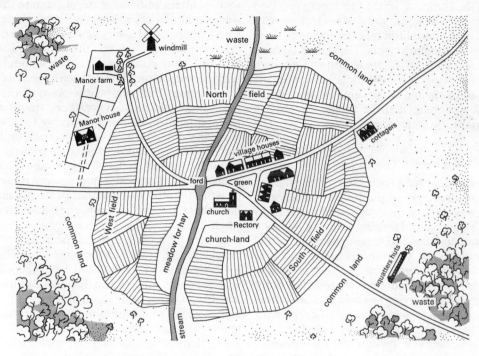

A village before enclosure

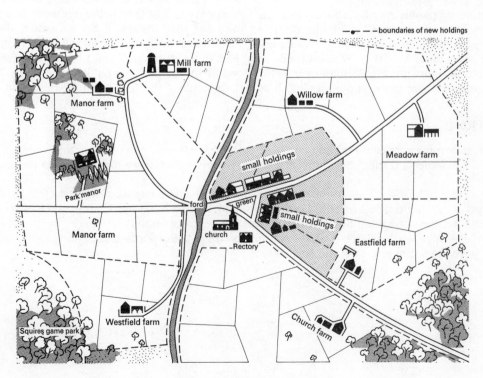

The village after enclosure

When this was done they re-allocated all the land including the common, so that each man received a compact farm of equal value of his former scattered holdings, plus a little bit extra to compensate for the loss of common rights. The commissioners also gave detailed instructions concerning such matters as fencing the new plots, drainage, the provision of roads and tracks and so forth. When their work was completed the village would have been permanently transformed.

The Effects of Enclosures

Enclosures undoubtedly benefited farming. They made proper drainage, crop rotation and the other new techniques easier to apply and they did away with much wastage of land. By bringing the common and wasteland under the plough they increased the cultivated area very considerably and they made it possible to grow more food in greater variety. the hedges and fences protected crops from the wind and straying animals, and since more fodder was grown it was possible to keep beasts through the winter. Fresh meat was therefore available at all times of the year and it was possible to build up improved breeds of cattle and sheep. Overall the enclosures greatly increased the efficiency of British agriculture and they were an important factor in enabling this country to feed its rapidly growing population.

The effects on people are a little harder to assess. Obviously with more food available everyone ultimately benefited from the changes, but enclosures did cause much hardship. Wealthy landlords found farming more profitable than ever before and they did well, but those whose previous hold-ings had been small often suffered. The cottagers and squatters who had no legal claim to their land were usually evicted altogether, while those people who had once had a very small holding in the open fields found that, despite the compensation they received, they could not carry on without the use of the common on which to keep a pig or a cow and a few geese. Farmers in this position often sold their smallholding to a wealthier neighbour and became landless labourers working for a wage on someone else's farm. It seems certain that enclosure was always followed by some transfer of land from the poorer to the richer farmers and it was probably this fact which prompted Arthur Young to write that 'by nineteen out of twenty inclosure bills the poor are injured, and some grossly injured'.

In general however the hardship caused by enclosure seems to have been exaggerated. The slump in farming which followed the Napoleonic Wars was probably the reason for the decline in the number of yeomen or small independent farmers, and some of the hardship in the countryside in the late eighteenth century was caused by the French Wars themselves and not by enclosures. By increasing the amount of cultivated land the enclosure movement almost certainly increased the amount of work available in the country districts, and may well have reduced the amount of poverty rather than added to it. All that can be said with certainty is that the enclosures were an upheaval, and for that reason, if for no other, they were unpopular with the ordinary countryman who had to live through them. Life was not necessarily worse for the majority but it was certainly different as a result of the Agricultural Revolution.

QUESTIONS

1. How was farming carried out in an open field village? What were the faults in this system?
2. What developments during the eighteenth century made it necessary for farmers to produce more food?
3. Write a short note about each of the following and say what important contribution they made to the progress of agriculture; Jethro Tull, Lord Townshend, Robert Bakewell, Charles and Robert Colling.
4. How did Arthur Young and Squire Coke spread the new ideas about farming?
5. Describe the process by which a village was enclosed by Act of Parliament.
6. What were the social effects of the enclosures?

6 CHANGES IN TRANSPORT

The tremendous industrial and agricultural changes outlined in the previous chapters would have been impossible without improvements in transport. Packhorses, which had served well enough to carry bales of cloth and small amounts of coal and grain in the days of domestic industry and open-field agriculture, could not cope with the much greater demands of the new factories and farms. Raw materials, fuel, manufactured goods and farm produce had to be moved from place to place in ever increasing quantities and improved transport was the only solution.

CANALS

The navigable rivers of this country had been used for generations to transport heavy goods, and in the early eighteenth century many of them were deepened and widened to increase their usefulness. These rivers played a very important part in the early stages of the industrial revolution (the Severn for example provided a valuable outlet for the industrial products of the West Midlands) but as a means of transport natural waterways had a number of disadvantages. To begin with they were not always in the right place when judged by the needs of industry, and it was often necessary to send goods by packhorse in order to reach the navigable portion of a river. In addition they were liable to flood or drought according to the season and thus were very unreliable. It was a logical step therefore to construct artificial waterways which would have none of these disadvantages.

James Brindley

The engineer associated with the early development of canals in this country is James Brindley, who was born at Tunstead in the Peak District of Derbyshire in 1716. Brindley was a remarkable man. He could hardly read or write, and to the end of his life he remained unable to spell the word

Brindley's Barton aqueduct.

James Brindley.

1766 he started work on the Trent–Mersey Canal, which was financed by Josiah Wedgewood, the pottery manufacturer, and a group or North Staffordshire businessmen including Earl Gower, Brindley's former employer. In 1771 while work on the Trent-Mersey Canal was still in progress, Brindley linked it to the River Severn by constructing the Staffordshire-Worcestershire Canal. In the same year Birmingham and Wolverhampton were connected with the Severn by the building of the Birmingham Canal across the Black Country to a junction with the Staffordshire and Worcestershire Canal at Aldersley. At this time Brindley was also working on the Droitwich Canal and numerous branch canals, and he was in constant demand as an expert to advise on canal projects all over the country. In 1772 overwork began to affect his health. In September of that year he caught a chill while out surveying the Caldon Branch of the Trent-Mersey Canal, and he died from the after-effects on September 27th, leaving numerous tasks to be completed by his brother in law Hugh Henshall, and his very able pupil Robert Whitworth.

'navigation' properly. And yet he was a practical engineer of genius. Working in the most unorthodox manner, judging levels by eye and going to bed for days at a time when some particularly tricky problem needed thinking out, he built hundreds of miles of canals, and made an enormous contribution to Britain's industrial development.

Brindley's sponsor was the eccentric Francis Egerton, 3rd Duke of Bridgewater who, it is said, decided to forget an unhappy love affair with the beautiful Elizabeth Gunning (who later became Duchess of Argyle) by throwing himself into the task of improving his Lancashire estates. In order to speed up the transport of coal from his mines at Worsley to Manchester, 17 kilometers away; he decided to build a canal and appointed Rrindley as his engineer. In this way the famous partnership between the two men began in 1759. At first people said that the Worsley scheme was mad and both Brindley and the Duke were ridiculed for even attempting it, but in 1761 when the Bridgewater Canal was opened the ridicule turned to admiration. The canal was a complete success, the cost of coal in Manchester was halved and both men were praised for their foresight. The Barton aqueduct which Brindley built to carry the canal across the River Irwell was hailed as the eighth wonder of the world.

After this success Brindley was constantly at work on canal projects until the end of his life. In 1762 he began to extend the Bridgewater Canal from Manchester to the Mersey at Runcorn, and in

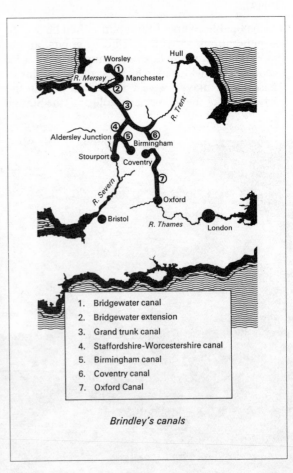

1. Bridgewater canal
2. Bridgewater extension
3. Grand trunk canal
4. Staffordshire-Worcestershire canal
5. Birmingham canal
6. Coventry canal
7. Oxford Canal

Brindley's canals

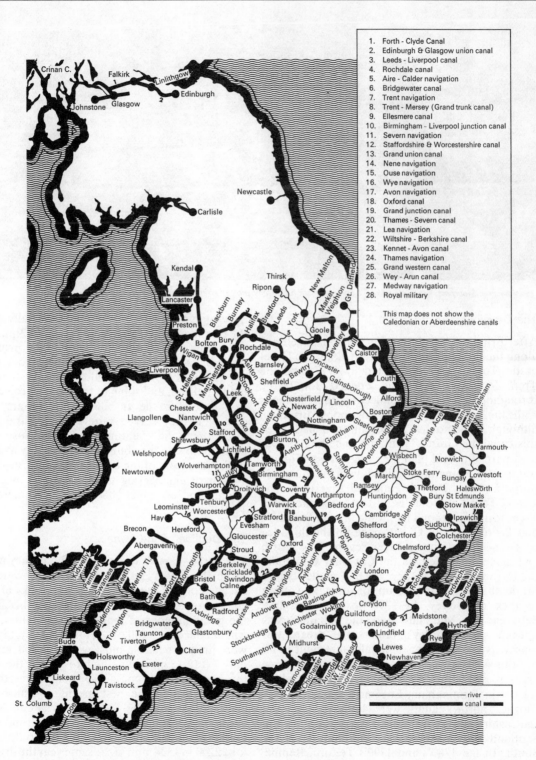

Inland navigation in Britain, about 1845

The canal basin at Stourport, Worcestershire — a communication centre of the early nineteenth century.

The Development of Canals

After Brindley's death the canal system developed along the lines he had forseen. Work on the Harecastle Tunnel was completed in 1777, and the Trent–Mersey Canal was opened for traffic throughout its length, connecting the Midlands with the growing port of Liverpool. Brindley, although he did not live to see it finished, had called this canal the Grand Trunk, because he had seen it as part of a bold plan for a huge cross of inland waterways joining the Midlands with the four main ports, London, Bristol, Hull and Liverpool. The Grand Trunk was one leg of the cross, the River Trent formed a second leg, while the Staffordshire and Worcestershire Canal made up the third leg by connecting with the River Severn. The fourth and much longer leg via the Coventry Canal and the Oxford Canal was surveyed by Brindley before his death, but it was held up for some time owing to lack of money. In 1790 however this link between the Midlands and the Thames was opened and Brindley's remarkable dream was reality. Numerous branch canals were built to fill out this skeleton system and the Midlands became criss-crossed with busy waterways, most of which started in Birmingham, England's 'canal capital'. Further north, canals were built in industrial Lancashire and Yorkshire, across the Pennines, in Scotland and in the agricultural counties of the South. In the 1780's and 1790's Telford, Rennie, Henshall, Whitworth and all the leading canal engineers were hard at work in different parts of the country. Money for all these projects was eagerly supplied by the public, especially during the period of 'canal mania', between 1792 and 1797, when there was a rush to invest in the profitable business of canal transport. As it turned out, not all the schemes were as sound as the investors were led to believe, and some of the canals projected at that time were never built, while others, particularly if they served purely agricultural areas, lost money and eventually fell into disuse. However, thanks to the abundance of money available in the last years of the eighteenth century, and the wealth of engineering talent at work, over 4800 kilometers of canal had been completed by 1800.

The Decline of the Canals

The early years of the nineteenth century proved to be the heyday of the canals. They were slow because of the need to go through locks at every change of level. They were expensive because of the great number of individual companies, all of which collected a toll over a long journey, and they were limited because most were constructed with only 7 ft (2.13 m) locks which restricted the size of the barges which could use them. Nevertheless, canals provided the best means of transporting heavy goods and the busy industrial canals were enormously profitable. Shares in the Grand Trunk Canal which had originally cost £100 could be sold for £2200 in 1824, and in the same year the dividend paid on a £100 share in the Loughborough Navigation was a fantastic £197. These £100 shares could be sold for £4600.

The situation became very different, however, when the railway companies were able to provide a quicker service, and since they could afford to lose money on freight and make it up on passenger receipts, they could always undercut the canal companies prices. As the railways spread so the canals declined. In 1840 a share in the Loughborough Navigation had dropped in value to £1500 and by 1872 they could be bought for £200. Other canals which had never been really successful simply became derelict, and it is only in our own day, with the renewed interest in canals for holiday purposes, that they are coming back into use.

The Importance of Canals

Whatever their fate in later years the canals contributed enormously to Britain's industrial expansion in the years between 1760 and 1840.

Manchester, Birmingham, the Potteries, the Black Country and many other industrial areas owe much of their early prosperity and growth to the inland waterways built by Brindley and his successors. The canals these men created were the chief arteries of the first phase of the industrial revolution, and the names Grand Trunk, Grand Union, Grand Junction indicate the importance which was attached to the water highways by the engineers who built them.

Bingley Five Rise locks at the eastern end of the Leeds and Liverpool canal in Yorkshire. The five locks lift the waterway about 18 metres.

ROADS

Although many people recognized the need to improve the roads in the eighteenth century progress was hampered by the out of date system under which they were maintained. A law passed in the reign of Queen Elizabeth I had placed responsibility for the upkeep of the highways in the hands of the parishes along their route. Each parish was expected to repair its own portion of the main road by ensuring that the men of the village did from four to six days unpaid work each year carrying out the necessary repairs under the supervision of a locally elected surveyor. Naturally the men objected to this forced labour and the work was generally badly done. It was this system of parish-maintained roads which created the sort of conditions which Arthur Young and many other eighteenth century writers described in their books.

Celia Fiennes, a well born lady who travelled all over England between 1685 and 1703, has left many vivid accounts of Britain's roads at the start of our period. She described those in South Yorkshire as 'difficult and narrow' and she was forced 'by reason on the steepness and hazard of the wayes' to hire a guide to travel through Derbyshire. In Norfolk Miss Fiennes travelled on a road 'which lay under water and is very unsafe for strangers to pass over by reason of the holes and quicksands and loose bottom', and she arrived at Dunstable after a difficult journey along 'a sad road, full of deep sloughs'. Sixty years later Arthur Young found that in many parts of the country things were pretty much the same. A passage from his *Southern Tour* (1768) illustrates very clearly the difficulty of moving heavy loads at that time. 'Of all the roads that ever disgraced this kingdom in the very ages of barbarism, none ever equalled that from Billericay to the King's Head at Tilbury. It is for near twelve miles so narrow that a mouse cannot pass by any carriage ... The ruts are of an incredible depth ... and to add to all the infamous circumstances which concur to plague a traveller, I must not forget eternally meeting with chalk-wagons, themselves frequently stuck fast, till a collection of them are in the same situation, that twenty or thirty horses may be tacked to each to draw them out one by one'.

Turnpike Trusts

Road improvements only became possible with the introduction of turnpike trusts. These were private companies which took over stretches of road from parishes, put them into a proper state of repair,

33

A mail coach passes through a toll gate. There was a £2 fine for the gate keeper if the gate was not open for the coach to pass without stopping.

then ran them as profit-making concerns by charging tolls to those wishing to travel over them. The first trust was authorized by Parliament in 1663 but initially they spread quite slowly. Only 400 appeared between 1700 and 1750, and the real advances came in the period after 1750 when the changes in industry and agriculture increased the need for improvement. Between 1750 and 1790 over 1500 turnpike trusts were set up, and gradually a network of good main roads began to appear, at least on trunk routes between the chief towns. By 1800 toll houses like the one illustrated here were becoming a familiar feature of the English countryside.

Road Engineers

The money which became available through tolls allowed the turnpike trusts to employ full-time engineers, and this led to important improvements in the technique of road building. These improvements are chiefly associated with three great engineers.

1. *'Blind Jack' Metcalf.* The first pioneer in this field was John Metcalf, who was born at Knaresborough in Yorkshire in 1717. Despite his handicap of total blindness, Metcalf led an interesting and adventurous life. He served against the Jacobites at the time of the 1745 rebellion, and then made a living as a carter and horse trader, experiencing at first hand the difficulties of travel in the north of England. In 1765 he won a contract to repair a three mile (about 5 km) section of the road from Boroughbridge to Harrogate and he began to put into practice the ideas which established his

reputation as an engineer. Various laws passed in the early eighteenth century had limited the weight of wagons, and a law of 1753 stated that no wagon was to have wheels less than nine inches (229 mm) in width in order to avoid making ruts. Metcalf realized, however, that it was not traffic but weather which was the real enemy of a good road surface. He therefore paid special attention to drainage and good foundations for his roads, and his first one proved strong and very efficient in service. As a result he soon found employment with other turnpike authorities, and between 1765 and his retirement in 1792 Metcalf built nearly 320 kilometres of good road in the most difficult Pennine country in Yorkshire, Lancashire and on the Cheshire–Derbyshire border. This amazing man, who surveyed his routes by walking over them tapping

John Metcalf.

a hollow stick and who was unable to see any of his own work, was responsible for the first good roads to be built in England since the days of the Romans.

2. *Thomas Telford.* Thomas Telford, who was born in Dumfrieshire in Scotland in 1757, is the second of the great trio of road builders. To begin with he established his reputation as a highly skilled stone mason in London and then became a road and bridge builder whilst surveyor to the Shropshire county authorities in 1787. In 1801 he was appointed engineer to the newly established government Commission for Highland roads and Bridges, and in that post he was responsible for the construction of nearly 1600 kilometres of road and over 100 bridges in Scotland. After completing work on the Glasgow to Carlisle road in 1814, Telford was appointed engineer to the important London–Holyhead road, the chief monument to his skill as a road builder. This magnificent highway with its gentle gradients and beautiful suspension bridges across the River Conway and the Menai Straits, was built to Telford's very high standards. The foundations were heavy and solid in order to stop the road shifting, and the firm surface was slightly cambered to allow the rain to drain off. Great care was taken to ensure good drainage and when the road was finished coaches could make the journey from London to Holyhead (then the chief port of departure for Ireland) in 27 hours. Telford was also a brilliant canal and harbour engineer and in the opinion of many

Thomas Telford.

experts he deserves to be ranked as Britain's greatest ever civil engineer. In 1818 when the Institute of Civil Engineers was founded, Telford's colleagues showed the respect they had for his ability by electing him its first president.

3. *John Macadam.* Macadam, who was also born in Scotland, at Ayr in 1756, is probably the best known of all the road engineers because he developed a method of surfacing roads with small granite chippings which still bears his name. Macadam returned to England in 1783 after making a considerable fortune in New York as a merchant, and began to work as an engineer with a number of

Telford's fine suspension bridge over the Menai Straits. He carried his extension of Watling Street from Shrewsbury to Holyhead.

John Macadam.

a Macadamized road. Smaller turnpike companies found that Macadam's roads were cheaper and quicker to build than the heavy roads suggested by Telford, and his methods came into general use. Macadam became adviser on roads to the Board of Agriculture and in 1827 he was appointed Surveyor-General of the Highways by the government, a post he held until his death in 1836. On Macadam's advice the General Highways Act has passed by Parliament in 1835, finally abolishing compulsory labour on the roads. Under the terms of the Act each parish was instead to levy a rate to pay for the proper upkeep of the highways.

The Golden Age of Coaching

Thanks to the work of the great road engineers, the turnpike trusts and the encouragement of such government departments as the Board of Agriculture and the General Post Office, Britain had more than 35 000 kilometres of good road by 1830. The express mail coaches, which travelled along 27 trunk routes radiating from London and regularly changed horses at the coaching inns which had sprung up along the main roads, could average from 16 to 19 kilometres an hour. Newcastle was only 40 hours from London, Birmingham a mere 12 and the London to Edinburgh journey, which had previously taken a fortnight, was reduced to 2 days. All this was a far cry indeed from conditions of travel in 1741 when John Metcalf refused a seat in a coach from London to Harrogate in Yorkshire saying he preferred to walk because he was in a hurry!

small turnpike companies. In 1815 he was appointed engineer to the important Bristol Turnpike Trust and there he was able to develop his revolutionary methods to the full. Macadam did not believe heavy foundations were necessary for a good road provided the surface was waterproof, and he laid his surface of small stones on a very light foundation or even straight onto dry earth. These stones were pounded down into a smooth surface by the traffic and the roads proved very hardwearing in practice. They also had some 'give' in them and it was found that horses became tired less quickly on

Conclusion

The canals and roads transformed inland transport in this country in the important years between 1760 and 1830. They made it possible for raw materials and manufactured goods to be moved more easily from place to place and allowed businessmen and salesmen to travel quickly about the country securing the orders and contracts which promoted our industrial expansion. We must remember, however, that both the canals and the roads had drawbacks and limitations and that they were not the only means of transport available at the time. In the early years of the Industrial Revolution coastal shipping played a vital part in Britain's economic growth by carrying passengers and really heavy loads, such as coal and china clay, between the ports. Before the appearance of a national network of railways the passage by sea was often the only practical means of transport between certain

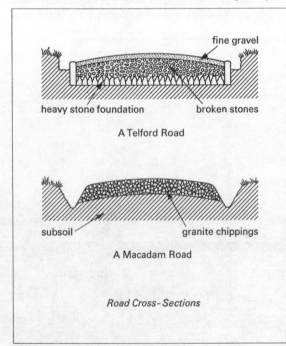

fine gravel

heavy stone foundation   broken stones

A Telford Road

subsoil   granite chippings

A Macadam Road

Road Cross-Sections

A stage coach.

parts of the country (it was, for example, the method chosen by the Stephensons to transport their famous locomotive *Rocket* from Newcastle to Liverpool in time for the Rainhill Trials in 1829) and coastal sailing vessels deserve to rank alongside the canal boats and stage coaches as important agents of the transport revolution in the late eighteenth century.

QUESTIONS

1. Why was it necessary to improve transport in the eighteenth century?
2. Write an account of the life and work of James Brindley.
3. Why did the British canals decline after 1840?
4. What was the importance of the canal network in the period from 1760 to 1840?
5. Describe and explain the condition of the roads in this country before the improvements came.
6. Describe the work of the following: Turnpike Trusts, John Metcalf, Thomas Telford, John Macadam.

SECTION 2

The Social Effects of the Industrial Revolution

In Section 1 we have been looking at the important economic changes involved in the Agricultural and Industrial Revolutions, and we have seen how these began quite slowly about halfway through the eighteenth century. Nearer the end of the century the process of change began to go ahead much more rapidly, chiefly because of the war against France which broke out in 1793. This war lasted with only short interruptions for 22 years, and it had enormous economic consequences. Factories were opened to manufacture arms, ammunition, uniforms and all the other requirements of war and in these factories the steam engine began to come into more widespread use. At the same time farmers rushed to enclose almost all that remained of the open fields and common land in order to grow more food, for the French blockade had led to an enormous increase in demand. The overall result, therefore, was a tremendous increase in the pace of both the agricultural and industrial changes we have already studied. By 1815, when the war ended, Britain was well on the way towards becoming a major industrial power—one which would soon be referred to as 'the workshop of the world'.

Naturally such far reaching economic changes affected the lives of many thousands of people. David Thomson, the historian, said that in 1815 'Britain was midway through the most far-reaching social transformation in her whole history' and in Section 2 we shall examine this transformation in detail by looking at social conditions in this country between 1800 and 1850.

7 BRITAIN IN THE EARLY NINETEENTH CENTURY

For many people the early years of the nineteenth century brought great ease and comfort. The landed aristocracy found that enclosures had increased the value of their estates and thus had given them new wealth to spend on fine houses and the fashionable way of life which was a feature of Regency England. Life was also good for many of those country gentlemen, a little further down the social scale, who actually farmed the great estates. Improvements in agriculture had also increased their rents and profits, and they had money to spend as never before. Many squires began to copy the social habits of the very rich and they sent their sons to school, and educated their daughters to be 'ladies'; a fashion which Gilray poked fun at in a famous cartoon published in 1809. Even the new race of northern factory owners and businessmen, who were generally less interested in display than the aristocracy, built solid, comfortable houses in the residential districts of the new towns and staffed them with servants. For these people then, the economic changes were beneficial.

For the great mass of ordinary people it is much harder to generalize. Much of the evidence is conflicting and unreliable, and among professional historians two schools of thought have grown up. Some have looked at the many examples of social distress in the early nineteenth century, at the insanitary conditions in the towns, at the plight of the agricultural workers, at the evidence of long hours and harsh conditions in the factories, and have concluded that living standards for the great mass of the workers fell, certainly until the 1840's. Others have disagreed with this view. They have pointed out that conditions in the days of domestic industry and open field agriculture were far from perfect and that much of the social distress was caused not by the Industrial and Agricultural Revolutions but by the French Wars which led to inflation, high prices and shortages. They also suggest that the changes in industrial methods and in farming technique made the essentials of life cheaper and more plentiful, and that they therefore contributed to a rise in the standard of living of the ordinary working man. The truth probably lies somewhere between these two extremes, but at the moment we cannot say that living standards rose in the early nineteenth century or that they declined, because we simply do not know. All we can do is to look at the conditions in which certain sections of the population lived at that time. It then becomes apparent that, whether standards had risen or not, life for a great many people was a constant struggle against poverty, and that compared to our own day the general level of working class life was extremely low.

Conditions in the Countryside

The French War had a disastrous effect in the country districts. The demand for home grown food encouraged rapid enclosure and the open fields and common land almost completely disappeared. This increased the numbers of people who experienced the sort of hardship we noted in Chapter 5, and swelled the class of landless labourers competing for jobs. The effect of this competition was to keep wages low at a time when prices were rising as a result of the war. Since countrymen were also losing the income they had once earned from domestic spinning and weaving, the effect was widespread rural poverty. The situation was so bad in Berkshire that as early as 1795, only two years after the outbreak of war, the county magistrates who were responsible for poor relief met at the Pelican Inn, Speenhamland, on the outskirts of Newbury, to work out a system of emergency aid.

The Speenhamland System

The Speenhamland System, which later spread all over the Southern counties, was based on the idea of a minimum wage which was fixed according to the price of bread at any given time. If a labourer earned less than the minimum he was to receive a dole from the parish poor fund to make up his wages to the required amount. Thus when the gallon loaf, weighing four kilogrammes, cost one shilling it was considered that a man needed three shillings a week to keep himself, and one shilling and sixpence extra for every member of his family. If he did not earn this amount he was given the dole to make his wages up to the appropriate figure. The system was an honest effort to improve the lot of farm labourers and it undoubtedly saved many families from outright starvation, but it had certain defects. Farmers, who bore the main burden of the increased poor rate, were reluctant to increase

wages and so the depressed condition of agricultural workers was prolonged. By 1815 thousands of farming families were living on charity. This had a demoralizing effect on men who had formerly had their independence under the old strip-farming system, and, coupled with the very harsh game laws which made it an offence punishable by death to be found with nets or snares, it caused great bitterness in the countryside. This bitterness sometimes showed itself in outbreaks of rick burning and violence. The generally poor conditions in the countryside led to a movement of population from many farming counties like Cheshire and Derbyshire into the nearby industrial towns.

The Factory Towns

Work was available in the new industrial towns in abundance, and people flocked into them in enormous numbers, attracted by the wages which were higher than those in the depressed agricultural districts, and also to escape from unemployment. Unfortunately many people found that they had only exchanged one set of problems for another.

Factory towns were of course a product of the Industrial Revolution. As manufacturing moved from the home into the factories workers had to be housed near to the places of work, and so in the very early years of the Industrial Revolution towns grew up in isolated areas near to fast-flowing

Gin Lane, engraved by Adlard from a Hogarth drawing – an indictment of the shocking London slums.

London slums in the mid-nineteenth century.

streams which were used to power the first mills. Cromford in Derbyshire, where Arkwright established his first water driven spinning mill in 1771, is a good example of an early factory village of this type. Later, when steam began to replace water power, factory production moved to the coalfields to be near supplies of fuel, and so the industrial districts of Lancashire, the West Riding of Yorkshire and Central Scotland began to grow very rapidly. Oldham in Lancashire, which was a village of about 400 people in 1760, had grown into a bustling industrial community of 12 000 when the first official census was taken in 1801. Nearby Bolton had developed from equally small beginnings into a town with 17 000 inhabitants, while Manchester with a population of 95 000 in 1801 was already established as the 'Cotton Capital' of northern England.

These towns sprang into existence before the days of town councils and planning authorities, and so their early growth was largely haphazard and unsupervised. Workers were accommodated in rows of mean, back-to-back houses run up by the factory owners at the least possible expense. Sanitation and water supplies were usually primitive and the overcrowded conditions and general lack of amenities quickly turned the rows of cottages into unhealthy slums. No provision was made until much later in the nineteenth century for parks, playgrounds and open spaces, and so work people lived out their lives amidst the constant grime and smoke of the nearby factory chimneys, with little or no chance of breathing clean, fresh air, or of escaping from the squalor of their surroundings. As the century progressed and the towns continued to grow rapidly (see table), outbreaks of cholera and typhoid became frequent and health standards in the towns were noticeably lower than in the surrounding country districts. The historian Sir Arthur Bryant says that by the 1840's 'the factory population of Lancashire and the West Riding was discoloured, stunted and seemed more like some ill-fated race of pygmies than normal human beings'.

The rapid growth of industrial towns in Britain in the first half of the nineteenth century.

	1801	1831	1861
Manchester and Salford	95 000	237 000	400 000
Leeds	53 000	123 000	172 000
Bradford	13 000	44 000	104 000
Bolton	17 000	42 000	61 000
Blackburn	12 000	27 000	65 000

Working conditions

It was not only the living conditions in the new towns which brought about the sort of results Sir Arthur Bryant described. Working conditions were also extremely harsh and contributed to the general hardship of town life. Hours were long and in most factories fourteen or sixteen hour shifts were quite normal. When the factory was really busy, shifts of eighteen hours might be worked because factory owners believed, in those fiercely competitive days, that the only way they could make a profit was to get the last ounce out of their work people. For these long hours wages were generally low. They were not as low as the depressed wages of the countryside, but still low enough to force whole families to work in order to live. Women and young children worked alongside the men putting in the same long hours, and 'strappers' were employed to walk round and keep the children awake at their work so that they did not fall into the machines. Many children worked these long shifts in cramped positions under the machines where they were sent to oil and clean parts which adults could not reach, and the result was that many of them grew up with twisted limbs and deformed bodies. John Hall, a Bradford worsted spinner, told the Select Committee of the House of Commons on Child Labour in 1832 that he knew personally of at least two hundred families in Bradford which had 'all deformed children', and this number could have been multiplied many times over in the textile areas as a whole. Lord Shaftesbury, the great factory reformer, described one group of crippled children he saw as a 'little crooked alphabet', and the suffering of the factory children is one of the saddest features of the early Industrial Revolution.

It must, however, be borne in mind that, judged by our standards, conditions of life had been much harder before the coming of the factories. The old cottage system of cloth manufacture had no restrictions on the use of children. The family living on a small-holding would have little more than the essentials of life.

Conditions in the Mines

Life in the coal mining areas was if anything even harder than in the large towns. The shabby mining villages were often in remote regions and there was no one to look after the miners' interests until their cause was taken up by Lord Shaftesbury later in the nineteenth century. For the most part the great coal owners regarded their miners as property rather than people, and it was not until the very end of the eighteenth century that Scottish miners ceased to be bound to their owners, like serfs under the feudal system in the Middle Ages. In mining too, hours were long and wages so low that whole families had to work. Young children were employed underground doing routine jobs like opening and closing ventilation doors, crouched for ten and twelve hours at a time in the darkness and damp of the pit bottom. The Royal Commission on

This print was used in the 1842 Mines Report.

Mines in 1842 found one child working underground at the age of three, although six years was the usual age at which children started working in the pits. Except in Northumberland and Durham, where pit ponies were used extensively, the hauling of coal underground was done by women and girls, and the picture on page 41, which is taken from the Government report on mining published in 1842, shows children crawling along the underground galleries pulling tubs of coal to which they are attached by chains, before carrying it to the surface a bag at a time. The effect of this sort of work on the health of the women and children involved can well be imagined.

Why People Accepted the Bad Conditions

People put up with the sort of living and working conditions which have been described because they had no choice. There was no unemployment pay or sick benefit in those days and a man either worked or he starved. It was not possible to seek improvements through combined action in trades unions because the Government, fearing they would breed revolution, had made these organizations illegal under the terms of the Combination Laws of 1799 and 1800. The Government itself was not prepared to do anything because it did not wish to seem weak by bowing to demands for reform, and because people in positions of authority genuinely believed that if they began to tamper with the economic system, for example by laying down scales of wages, then the whole system might collapse. It was better, so they believed, to encourage competition without any government interference. This 'Laissez-faire' (see glossary) idea, first put forward by Adam Smith in his book *Wealth of Nations* (See Chapter 11), held up many much needed reforms in the first part of the nineteenth century.

The only possible outlet for working class discontent, therefore, was violence and in years of bad harvests there were outbreaks of machine breaking and general lawlessness by men who claimed to be the followers of Ned Ludd, a legendary figure who was said to live in Sherwood forest. The Luddites, many of whom were hand craftsmen who felt that machines were taking away their livelihoods, were particularly active during the bad years 1810 to 1812 but they achieved nothing. The leaders were rounded up and very severely punished and the majority of the working population made the best of things and waited for better times.

Many were helped in this patient acceptance of things by their strong religious faith. In the 1740's John Wesley had begun his work of preaching and teaching among the poor of the mining areas and the growing towns and by the time of his death in 1791 he had converted thousands of people to Methodism. This strong but simple faith, which Wesley preached so powerfully during fifty years of ceaseless travelling about England, taught that every human being mattered to God and that even the poorest and most humble man had value in God's eyes. It gave men self respect, encouraged the virtues of thrift and good workmanship (something Josiah Wedgwood noted among his Methodist potters in Staffordshire) and above all gave people the hope of something better, if not in this life, then at least in the next. The social effect of these teachings was enormous. The growth of Methodism is probably one of the reasons why there was no revolution in Britain during the bad years of the early Industrial Revolution. Critics of Wesley would say that by teaching patience and acceptance he did not do the poor a real service but there can be no doubt that Methodism provided large numbers of individuals with spiritual comfort by giving their hard lives some meaning and that it was a powerful social force.

Post War Distress 1815–1822

Any hope that the end of the Napoleonic Wars would bring prosperity was doomed to disappointment because the peace of 1815 was followed by a serious slump. Factories making war goods closed down and threw their employees out of work. Thousands of soldiers and sailors came home from the war looking for work and swelled the number of unemployed, causing such keen competition for jobs that factory owners were able to reduce wages and still get all the men they needed. At the same time the landowners who controlled Parliament looked after their own interests by passing the Corn Law of 1815, which stopped the importation of foreign corn until English farmers were getting 80s. a quarter for home produced grain. This very selfish act of Parliament protected the farmers, but when harvests were bad it was liable to cause distress in the manufacturing districts by pushing up the price of bread. Equally selfish and equally hard on the poor was Parliament's decision in 1816 to abolish the war-time income tax. This tax had fallen most heavily on those best able to pay it, namely the rich, and for this reason the rich, acting through Parliament, decided to get rid of it. The revenue which it had provided was still required however, and so a series of indirect taxes on everyday articles such as candles was introduced in its place. These naturally fell most heavily on the poor.

Not surprisingly, therefore, the years after 1815 were marked by an increase in violence. There were riots in London at Spa Fields in 1816 and more serious disturbances in the north in the following year. The Government, which was still frightened that the ideas of the French Revolution might take root in England, countered these outbreaks with fiercely repressive measures designed to stamp out all trouble and stifle all criticism. People were imprisoned without trial; punishments in the courts became more severe, and famous critics of the government, like the farming journalist William Cobbett, were forced to flee the country. Sections of the working class now began to add to their demands for better conditions a further demand for the reform of Parliament to allow ordinary people some say in the way the country was run. Meetings were held up and down the country to promote this idea, and one of these, held in St. Peter's Fields, Manchester in 1819, ended in tragedy. The local magistrates panicked when they saw the size of the crowd which had assembled to hear speeches by 'Orator' Hunt and other noted agitators, and they ordered the cavalry to ride in and break up the demonstration. In the scuffle which followed eleven people were killed (including three women and a child) and several hundred were injured. This 'Peterloo Massacre' made the Government more unpopular than ever and this led to a new wave of unrest, which was countered by the Government with harsh new laws called the 'Six Acts'. These 'Gag Acts', as they are often called, extended the right to search private houses; increased the stamp duty on newspapers so as to force workingmen's periodicals out of their reach by making them too expensive; made it possible for magistrates to convict without a jury; increased the penalties for writing critically of the Government in the press; made it more difficult for opposition groups to hold public meetings and stiffened the penalties for drilling and possessing private arms. These measures, and the Government's use of spies like the notorious Oliver, who had deliberately stirred up an outbreak among the Derbyshire unemployed in 1817 in order to arrest the ringleaders, made the authorities tremendously unpopular. It seemed to many people

The Manchester Yeomanry charging the mob at Peterloo in 1819 – from a cartoon by George Cruikshank.

A Peeler in 1829.

A more settled and confident look about this policeman in the mid-nineteenth century.

at this time that the country was moving towards revolution.

Better Times 1822–1830

Fortunately in the early 1820's things began to improve and the danger of serious disorders faded. About this time trade began to pick up after the post war slump and some of the new prosperity filtered down to the working population. After 1822, when new men came into the Government, some of the very harsh laws were relaxed, and Robert Peel, the Home Secretary, did important work reducing the severe punishments for small crimes which had made the law hated rather than respected. Peel also introduced the Metropolitan Police Force, and when other cities began to copy this idea the risk of future tragedies like Peterloo was reduced, because unarmed civilian police became responsible for law and order instead of the Army. In 1824 Francis Place secured the repeal of the Combination Laws. This made trade union activity possible and enabled working men to start organizing themselves to demand better conditions (See Chapter 9). At the same time William Huskisson, the new President of the Board of Trade, began to reduce customs duties on many foreign imports, which promoted trade and created more work in the factories.

By 1830 conditions had improved considerably in comparison with the bad years immediately after the war, but we must not imagine that all hardship had disappeared. A bad harvest could still reduce working families, especially in the country districts, to starvation level and the Government was still unsympathetic to many genuine grievances. When the starving field labourers of southern England rioted in 1830 and demanded a basic wage of two shillings and sixpence a day ($12\frac{1}{2}$p), troops were used to put the rising down, nine of the ringleaders were hanged, 457 were transported to Australia and about the same number were put in prison in this country. There was still a long way to go before the ordinary working man received a fairer share of the new wealth which industrialization was bringing to this country.

QUESTIONS

1. What effects did the French Wars have upon life in the countryside after 1793?
2. Describe the development of the early factory towns.
3. Describe working conditions in the factories and the mines in the early nineteenth century.
4. Describe the social distress in Britain after 1815.

8 AN AGE OF REFORM: BRITAIN 1830—1850

The Parliamentary System

For generations political power in this country lay in the hands of a small group of aristocratic landlords who sat in the House of Lords and packed the House of Commons with their supporters by nominating them for the 'rotten' and 'pocket' borough seats (see glossary) they controlled. While England remained an agricultural country there was very little criticism of the system. Most people in the country worked on the land and it seemed right that the laws should be made by people who were connected with farming themselves and who possessed in addition the necessary education and experience to govern properly.

The Industrial Revolution changed all this. The wealthy factory owners and merchants who made up the new industrial middle class were not satisfied with a government composed of country squires and rich landlords, and they began to demand that Parliament should be reformed to give them a voice in the nation's affairs. They particularly wanted the right to vote in Parliamentary elections and they also demanded that Parliamentary seats should be given to the new industrial towns.

For the first thirty years of the nineteenth century all these demands met with a blank refusal. The Tory party, which was in a majority in Parliament, was determined to allow no alteration to the system. With the violence and bloodshed of the French Revolution still fresh in their minds, the Tories thought that to give in to any demand for Parliamentary reform was the surest way of encouraging similar revolutionary outbreaks in England. They therefore set themselves solidly against change, and it was only after 1830, when the Tory party fell from power, that progress was possible.

Parliamentary Reform

The Whig party which made up the new government in 1830 was composed almost entirely of landowners, but unlike the Tories they believed that reform was necessary. As a result they passed the Great Reform Act of 1832. This important law transferred 146 rotten and pocket borough seats to the new industrial towns and more heavily populated counties, and gave the vote to the better off sections of the industrial middle classes in the towns. Merchants and manufacturers now joined the landowners in a political partnership. There was nothing in the Act for the working class and, as we shall see (page 55), their disappointment was soon expressed in the Chartist movement. Indirectly, however, ordinary people did benefit from the changes made in 1832. The reformed House of Commons was prepared to accept some measure of change and it was ready to listen to the views of enlightened individuals who pointed out the need for social reform.

Reformers

Not surprisingly, in view of the bad conditions which existed at the time, the nineteenth century is rich in reforming personalities; people who devoted their lives to the task of improving social conditions. Some were inspired by their Christian faith, some by ideas which we should now call socialism and

Robert Owen, the pioneer factory reformer and socialist.

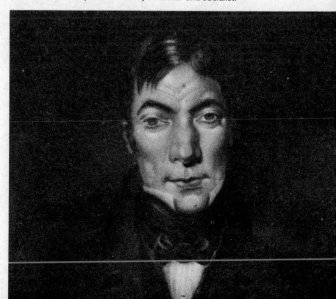

Owen's labour note, the value of it being based on hours of work.

New Lanark Mills, contrary to what a lot of people expected, still made very handsome profits.

Unfortunately few factory owners followed Owen's lead at the time and so, as we shall see (page 52), he threw himself into various schemes for co-operative production and trading which have earned for him the title 'the father of English socialism'. These schemes, like his Grand National Consolidated Trades Union (see page 54) were unsuccessful and Owen regarded his own life as a failure. He did prove at New Lanark, however, that factory reform was possible, and he was a source of inspiration to those who took up the campaign where he left off.

Lord Shaftesbury's origins were as aristocratic as Owen's were humble. He was born into a rich Tory landowning family but his deep religious beliefs and the appalling conditions of the tenants on his father's estates, caused him to turn his back on his own class and devote his life to the poor. From the time he took over the leadership of the factory reform movement in Parliament in 1833 until his death, Shaftesbury was in the forefront of almost every battle for social reform. He played a large part in securing the passage of the Factory Acts of 1833, 1844 and 1850 and the Mines Act of 1842. He was the chairman of Royal Commissions which investigated such matters as public health and the treatment of the insane, and he campaigned for years on behalf of the boy chimney sweeps until he succeeded in getting the wicked practice of sending them up hot, suffocating chimneys stopped by Parliament. He also set up 'ragged schools' in many of our large industrial towns and was one of the first to encourage Dr.

other, like F. D. Maurice, Charles Kingsley and the other leaders of the mid-century Christian-Socialist movement, by a combination of the two, but broadly their aims were similar. They wished to remove the worst features of the industrial system they saw around them. Two of the most outstanding reformers of that period were Robert Owen and Lord Shaftesbury.

Robert Owen was the pioneer of factory reform. He rose from humble beginnings to become the manager of the New Lanark Mills in Scotland and there in 1800 he began the experiment which has made him famous. Owen took over a typical early nineteenth century mill in which the workers were underpaid, overworked and where a large proportion of them were very young children. In a very short time Owen entirely transformed this situation. He reduced hours, raised wages and refused to employ any children under ten years of age. He improved the factory itself and nearby laid out a model village of good houses for his workpeople to live in. He sold good quality food at cost price at a company shop and also provided a school and a community centre. Owen's employees responded to this good treatment by working hard so that the

The schoolroom in Robert Owen's model village at New Lanark in Scotland. The use of pictures and maps was in advance of the times.

Barnado in his plans to establish homes for orphans. It is fitting that this great man should still be remembered as 'the children's friend'.

The Age of Reform

As a result of the reforming zeal of men like Shaftesbury and of the more liberal outlook of the reformed House of Commons, many outstanding problems were tackled in the years between 1830 and 1850.

a. *Factory Laws.* As we have seen the need to reform factory conditions was obvious to people like Robert Owen from the very beginning of the factory age, and two laws were passed by Parliament very early in the nineteenth century. In 1802 Robert Peel the elder, the father of the future Prime Minister, persuaded parliament to pass the Health and Morals of Apprentices Act, which was intended to limit the hours and improve the working conditions of pauper apprentices; and in 1819 Peel and Owen together forced through a Factory Act which was to do the same for free children. Unfortunately neither of these acts was successful. No proper arrangements were made to ensure that the laws were obeyed and factory owners simply ignored them.

The first really effective factory law was the Factory Act of 1833. This law was passed after a vigorous campaign in the north of England led

Lord Shaftesbury, the great social reformer often called 'the children's friend'.

A chimney sweep's boy in 1853. Boys like this actually went up the chimneys to sweep out the soot by hand.

by Richard Oastler, a land agent from Huddersfield, Michael Sadler a Tory M.P., John Fielden a millowner from Todmorden in Lancashire, and Lord Shaftesbury. Oastler's letters on 'Yorkshire Slavery' published in the *Leeds Mercury* in 1830 aroused considerable public feeling in favour of reform and Sadler was able to arrange for an official committee of inquiry into child labour. In 1833 Lord Shaftesbury took over the leadership of this committee and his skill in presenting its shocking findings made reform possible.

The 1833 Factory Act applied to all textile factories (except silk mills) and stated that;
a. No children under nine were to work at all.
b. Children from nine to thirteen were to work no more than 9 hours per day.
c. Young persons from thirteen to eighteen were to work no more than 12 hours per day.
d. The terms of the act were to be enforced by a body of factory inspectors specially set up for the purpose.

This last point was perhaps the most important. From 1833 onwards the factory regulations had to be obeyed and the 1833 Factory Act is therefore a landmark in English social history.

The demand for new factory laws continued. The act of 1833 was seen as only a start and the main aim of the reformers became the ten hour

Part of the first page of Charles Kingsley's 'The Water Babies'. This book was written to expose the evils of using children as chimney sweeps.

He was the chairman of the Royal Commission set up in 1840 to examine working conditions in the mines, and it was the report of this commission, illustrated by pictures like the one on page 41, which persuaded Parliament to act. After a bitter struggle in the House of Lords, where Lord Londonderry and the other great coal owners did everything they could to hold up the bill, the Mines Act became law in 1842. This Act stopped the employment of women and young people underground, and stated that no children under ten years of age were to be employed in the mining industry at all. The commission had found evidence that accidents had been caused by putting young children in charge of winding gear, and so the Act also made it a rule that no person under the age of 15 should be put in charge of machinery. In 1850 the Mines Act was followed up by another act which set up a separate body of mine inspectors.

c. *The Poor Law Act 1834*. In 1834 the Whig government decided to tackle the pressing problem of the poor law. They did so in what was becoming the approved manner: a Royal Commission was set up and then a law was passed based on the Commission's recomendations. Edwin Chadwick, the chairman of the Poor Law Commission, was a follower of the philosopher Jeremy Bentham. Bentham believed that all laws should bring 'the greatest good to the greatest number' and should not benefit only one small section of the community. He believed that laws should really work and if

Edwin Chadwick, the great Poor Law and Public Health Reformer.

working day. To this end agitation continued both inside and outside Parliament and gradually new laws were introduced. The 1844 Factory Act fixed a maximum twelve hour working day for women and also made regulations for the fencing of dangerous machinery. The Fielden Factory Act, or 'Ten Hour Bill', of 1847 achieved the ten hour working day for women and young persons and seemed like a triumph for the ten hour movement. Unfortunately the triumph was short lived. Factory owners got round the Act by working women and young people in shifts or relays and so a further law was necessary in 1850. This was a compromise hammered out in Parliament by Shaftesbury and the factory owners in which they agreed to stop relay-working in return for an extra half hour on the working day. Factories were to open from 6 a.m. to 6 p.m. or 7 a.m. to 7 p.m. during which time the workpeople were to have one and a half hours off for meals. This surrender of half an hour to the factory owners made Shaftesbury very unpopular for a time, but the Factory Act of 1850 did achieve its object. By limiting the time factories could stay open it effectively reduced the hours for adult male workers as well as ending the practice of relay-working. These Acts only related to textile mills, but other factories in other industries began to fall into line after 1850.

b. *The Mines Act 1842.* Parallel with the movement for factory reform there was also a demand for improvements in the coal mining industry, and here again Lord Shaftesbury played a leading part.

A visitor reads an improving text to the inmates of a workhouse.

they did not, that they should be scrapped.

Chadwick brought this Benthamite way of looking at things to his task of investigating the system of poor relief. He found that the arrangements made at Speenhamland (see page 39) had become widespread over much of the country, and that the results had been unfortunate. Wages had been forced down, thousands of working men were living on charity and a very heavy burden had been placed upon that section of the community which paid the poor rate. The system did not bring the greatest good and, since it was very badly administered, it was also extremely inefficient. Chadwick therefore proposed that it should be changed.

The Poor Law Amendment Act of 1834, which was based on the Commission's report, abolished the Speenhamland System of outdoor relief. Able-bodied persons who needed assistance in future were to receive it in workhouses. These were to be deliberately made more unpleasant than the most unpleasant kind of life outside in order to force people to fend for themselves. Inside the workhouses families were split up into separate male and female wards and the work provided for the inmates to do was dirty and usually very boring. The workhouses themselves were built in every large parish or group of smaller parishes (Poor Law Unions) and under the terms of the Act they were controlled by locally elected Boards of Guardians. The whole poor law system was directed from London by Chadwick and two other full time Poor Law Commissioners appointed by the act.

The new 'Poor Law Bastilles', as they became known, were hated by the poor who lived in constant dread of being forced into the workhouse by ill health or a spell of unemployment. But the system did work, although applied more often in the south of England than in the north. The cost of poor relief was halved, and employers after 1834 were forced to pay at least a minimum living wage otherwise they lost their workers altogether. The arrangements made by Chadwick lasted with slight modifications for almost a hundred years, until the reform of the poor law in 1929.

d. *Local Government.* Another problem which the Whigs tackled in the 1830's was the lack of government in many of the new towns. Some of these big industrial centres were run by out-dated closed corporations which were a relic of the middle ages, while others, which had grown up where no town had existed before, had no local government at all, except for the overworked local J.P. or Lord of the Manor. The solution to this problem was the Municipal Corporations Act of 1835. This act provided for elected local councils in the towns and empowered these councils to levy a local tax or rate to finance town improvements. All householders were to pay the rate and in return they were to receive the right to vote at local elections. The new town councils greatly encouraged local civic pride, and it was not long before many of them were asking Parliament for permission to erect town halls and other public buildings. They also began to provide parks, libraries and other amenities which went a long way towards improving the quality of town life in this country.

e. *Public Health.* Concern over conditions in the new industrial towns also prompted some improvements in the field of public health. These improvements were badly needed. There was evidence that slum conditions in the new towns were allowing new killer diseases, like tuberculosis, to gain ground as fast as old ones, like smallpox, were being conquered, and the high death rate among slum dwellers in the cholera outbreak of 1831 emphasized the health hazard of bad housing. A number of careful surveys made in the 1840's also pointed to the need for action. The 'Report on the Sanitary Condition of the Labouring Population of Great Britain' compiled by Chadwick and the Poor Law commissioners in 1842 was filled with details of the appalling conditions in which thousands of families lived, and these findings were borne out by the separate enquiries conducted by Dr. Southwood-Smith. In 1846 Peel appointed a committee of inquiry to look at the 'Large Towns and Populous Districts' and this body confirmed the need for public health laws. The result was the Public Health Act of 1848 which set up a full time Board of Health, whose first members included Chadwick, Southwood-Smith and Lord Shaftesbury. The Board was given power to set up local boards in places where the death rate exceeded 23 per 1000 or where 10% of the population asked for one. These boards were to be responsible for the provision of fresh water supplies, sewerage schemes, matters relating to housing and so on.

The Penny Black postage stamp introduced in 1840 by Rowland Hill.

The Board of Health did not really achieve all that was hoped of it. Chadwick's overbearing manner aroused stiff local opposition to many of his ideas and the resistance of slum land-lords interfered with the work of many boards. As a result the Board of Health in London was wound up in 1858. Its work did carry on at a local level, however, and at least a start had been made. The 1848 Public Health Act laid a foundation on which the much more successful public health laws of the 1860's and 1870's could build.

f. *Other Reforms.* Factory conditions, the poor law, public health and town government were among the major domestic problems tackled between 1830 and 1850, but they were not the only matters to receive Parliament's attention. In 1833 the Whig government crowned the life's work of William Wilberforce by abolishing slavery in the British Empire—just a few weeks before the great reformer's death. In the same year Parliament accepted some responsibility for education for the first time, by making a grant of £20 000 to the National Society and the British and Foreign Schools Society; two voluntary bodies which provided much of the limited elementary education available to ordinary people in those days. This grant was increased to £30 000 in 1839 enabling the societies to open more schools and spend more money on teacher training. In the following year another important improvement was introduced when the government took up the suggestion of Rowland Hill, a former post office official, and established the Penny Post.

We shall examine the reforms in connection with trade in a separate chapter (page 68), but if the free trade measures of Peel which culminated in the repeal of the Corn Laws in 1846 are added to the catalogue of improvements we have looked at in this chapter, it can be seen that the period from 1830 to 1850 is rightly termed 'an age of reform'.

QUESTIONS

1. How was the Parliamentary system changed by the Reform Act of 1832?
2. Describe the work of Robert Owen and Lord Shaftesbury.
3. What progress was made in factory reform between 1800 and 1850?
4. Describe the Poor Law of 1834 and say why it was very unpopular among ordinary people in this country.
5. What important reforms in local government and public health took place between 1830 and 1850?

9 SELF HELP

The preceding chapter showed how Parliament, reluctantly and after much prodding by individual reformers, began to control some of the worst aspects of working conditions. Parallel to the exertions made on behalf of the working classes were the efforts made by the working men and their leaders to improve their standard of life themselves. Typical of the thinking of the period was Samuel Smiles's book *Self Help*. In it he expressed the belief that any poor man had a remedy for his poverty in his own hands. Hard work, thrift and determination would enable a man to do anything. 'God helps those who help themselves. Go thou and do likewise.'

Courses of Action

Working class leaders saw three main possibilities.
a. Workers could combine in trades unions and by means of weight of numbers and organization bring pressure to bear on their employers.
b. They could try to gain parliamentary influence and thus make sure that much-needed laws concerning work and living conditions were passed.
c. They could ignore both the employers and Parliament and organize a system of work which gave the workers the profits from factories and shops, and which would be under the direct control of the workers themselves. This would be achieved by the creation of co-operatives.

Co-operatives

The first half of the nineteenth century saw a number of attempts at schemes of co-operation. The idea of establishing co-operatives was attractive to the working classes because they felt that it was well within their capabilities to do so, as well as a feeling that a co-operative system could be directly beneficial. There seemed to be a greater chance of success in this course of action than

Samuel Smiles, the author and prophet of Self-Help.

Toad Lane Store Rochdale, the first shop of the present day Co-operative Society.

in trying to persuade Parliament to take action to control hours of work and rates of pay.

When we think of the term 'co-operative' today we think of the Co-operative Wholesale Society with its branches up and down the country. The situation was very different in the early years of the nineteenth century. There was no general organization. Some societies concerned themselves with providing educational opportunities. Others aimed to sell directly to their members and thus eliminate the 'middleman' who somehow got in between the producer of an article and the person buying it. Some organizations specialized in co-operative production, members making articles for themselves. There were over five hundred of these types of society in 1832.

Some co-operatives tried to help each other by setting up a central shop for their goods, known as a co-operative bazaar. Robert Owen, a firm believer in co-operation, helped to organize this, but the idea did not last long. There was no protection for funds, and dishonesty wrecked a number of societies. Not until the 1840's did there

appear a co-operative which was capable of surviving the early difficulties.

In 1844 some Rochdale flannel weavers got together and formed the 'Rochdale Society of Equitable Pioneers'. They aimed to build or purchase houses for their members, to rent land, to manufacture articles, to 'arrange the powers of production, distribution, education, and government'. It was, however, their first aim which has lasted. This was to establish a store for the sale of provisions, clothing etc.

It was no coincidence that they were weavers. The power loom had struck at the livelihood of hand weavers. They were, however, still self-employed and thus outside the factory system. They wanted above all to avoid the ordinary type of shop, run by an individual who pocketed the profits. Their aim was co-operation.

The subscription was fixed at 1p a week and when sufficient money had been collected, a warehouse was rented in Toad Lane. Anyone buying from the Toad Lane store received a dividend coming from the profit which would normally have gone into the pocket of the private shopkeeper. By the 1860's there were 450 stores with 90 000 members, and in 1863 the English Co-operative Wholesale Society was set up so that these stores could buy from a co-operative producer. A Scottish Society followed five years later.

A curious thing had happened however. The co-operative stores had not replaced the private shopkeeper and the middleman. They had become instead, an alternative form of shop within the system they had hoped to replace.

The Trade Unions

The formation of trade unions was perhaps the most obvious form of self help. Indeed the idea of forming associations for people employed in the same trade or profession goes back far beyond the days of the Industrial Revolution. Craftsmen working in gold, silver, and leather had formed guilds in medieval days. They had drawn up sets of rules governing hours of work, payment to members who were unable to work because of sickness, and had controlled standards of craftsmanship. Then in the eighteenth century Spitalfields weavers in London had banded together, as had the woollen combers in Yorkshire, and in 1792 Oldham cotton spinners started to run a benefit club.

The first real landmark in the development of trade unions was a negative one. In 1799 and in

Agricultural workers meet secretly to organize a trade union, a very similar type of proceeding to that which earned the men of Tolpuddle sentences of transportation.

1800 the Government passed several Acts which, taken together, have become known as the Combination Laws. These Acts forbad workmen (and, incidentally, their employers) from forming any associations. Britain was in the middle of a bitter struggle with France and the government used this as an excuse to ban unions of working men. On paper the banning of similar associations of the employers looked a fair arrangement. In fact the employees needed the right to form associations or trade unions far more than their masters, for only by combinations could individual workmen hope to bring pressure to bear on their employers.

It is important to realize that the Combination Acts were aimed at a very different type of association to that of the old guilds, which often consisted of self employed craftsmen. These infant trade unions were combinations of men often employed in factories connected with the textile industry. They were not their own masters. Their hours of work, their rates of pay and their conditions of work were matters over which they had little control.

For a time trade unions were forced to act like secret societies. Anyone concerned in their activities ran the risk of prosecution under the Combination Act, and earlier laws, against conspiracy. An example of this occurred in 1810 when some of the compositors of the *Times* newspaper (the men who set up the type) received sentences ranging up to ten years imprisonment. 'Bloody Black Jack' Sylvester who sentenced the men said 'you have been convicted of a most wicked conspiracy to injure ... those very employers who gave you bread ... the frequency of such crimes ... demand that a severe example should be made.'

It was obvious that little could be done until these Acts were repealed. The problem was how poor and ill educated working men could achieve such a repeal. Fortunately there were men in better circumstances who were prepared to work for this end.

Francis Place and Joseph Hume

Place, the son of a bailiff, had been apprenticed to a tailor and had gradually worked his way up to the position of master tailor. He was able to open his own shop in 1799. The little parlour at the back of this establishment in Charing Cross road contained a fine library and became the meeting place of men interested in reform, particularly in the repeal of the Combination Laws.

One of the men who came regularly to the little shop in Charing Cross was Joseph Hume. He had been a surgeon in India, and in 1812 he became a Member of Parliament. Hume's position as an M.P. was of great value, and in 1824 he managed to get a committee of Parliament appointed to look into the question of the Combination Acts. Place gave him enthusiastic support for he hoped that, if these Acts were repealed, workers would be less concerned with secret meetings and midnight gatherings, and would concentrate instead on securing the right to vote for all working men. In Place's eyes this was more important than building up the trade union movement.

The Parliamentary Committee heard evidence from masters and workers. In Place's words: 'the delegates from the working people had reference to me and I opened my house to them ... I examined and cross examined them; took down the leading particulars of each case, and then arranged the matters as briefs for Mr. Hume'.

The work bore fruit, for Parliament repealed the laws in 1824, but subsequently when faced with a sudden wave of strikes, they considered reimposing them. Only frantic work by Place and Hume

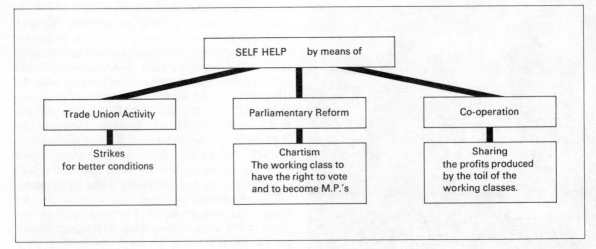

SELF HELP	by means of	
Trade Union Activity	Parliamentary Reform	Co-operation
Strikes for better conditions	Chartism The working class to have the right to vote and to become M.P.'s	Sharing the profits produced by the toil of the working classes.

prevented this. Nevertheless they could not prevent Parliament from passing an Act which, although it allowed workmen the right to form trade unions, in fact made it very difficult to call a strike without running the risk of being accused of forming a conspiracy.

Despite this handicap it was at least possible to organize trade unions openly, although some still carried on with the rigmarole of secret oath-taking among shrouded figures and skeletons. These had originally been designed to impress new members—relics of the illegal days of the trade unions.

In 1829 John Doherty, an Irishman, established a cotton spinners union in Manchester. He became more ambitious and set up the National Association for the Protection of Labour with its own newspaper. Each union had to pay £1 on joining. Unfortunately the idea was too ambitious and by 1832 the union had collapsed.

A similar fate befell the efforts of the miners of Northumberland and Durham to form a union. Their association was so completely broken by the masters that the miners' leader, Tommy Hepburn, could only get work by promising never to join a union again.

Other unions appeared, including one composed of builders (bricklayers) which had some success. This was overshadowed by the grandest scheme yet, that of the Grand National Consolidated Trades Union. Behind this impressive title lay, yet again, the driving force of Robert Owen. Owen's importance in achieving a measure of factory reform was seen in the previous chapter, but he regarded the Factory Acts as only tampering with the evils of capitalism. He thought it would be far better to sweep away the capitalist system of production altogether. Owen believed that if only all workers would unite then they could break the power that the employers had over them. At first it looked as though Owen's plan would succeed. In a matter of weeks over half a million members had been enrolled. The various trades or 'lodges' were grouped into districts, and each district sent a representative to a trades parliament. The lodges were to pay a levy which would be used for a strike and unemployment fund.

The Government was alarmed, and looked for some way of breaking the Grand National. In fact the Union was top-heavy and the various sections did not co-operate in the way that Owen had hoped. It would have fallen to pieces anyway, but the Government was able to precipitate this in 1834.

The Tolpuddle Martyrs

The wretched conditions of the country workers in the early 1830's resulted in the strikes and riots led, apparently, by the mysterious Captain Swing. The riots were crushed, and, as we have seen, many of the men involved were hanged or transported. Despite this, the news of the creation of the Grand National encouraged some villagers of Tolpuddle in Dorsetshire, led by George Loveless, to form a trade union and to ask for instructions on procedure from the Grand National. Their main aim was to lift their wages from seven shillings to ten shillings a week, a sum already being paid in neighbouring areas. Unfortunately the old habits of secret oath-taking persisted. A life-sized figure of a skeleton featured in their initiation ceremony and this gave the Government its opportunity. An Act of 1797 prohibiting the taking of unlawful oaths was used against the Tolpuddle men and seven were sentenced to be transported for seven years.

The Chartist uprising at Newport in 1839. It was here that George Shell died.

Unlike some of the grim events of these years there was a happier outcome. A committee based in London managed to get the sentences reduced. The men returned in 1837 and public subscription provided them with small farms of their own. But trade unionism had received a heavy blow. The year of the Tolpuddle case saw the collapse of the Grand National. Union activity did not cease of course, but working men began to consider the possibility of following another course of action, the one dear to the heart of Francis Place, that of gaining Parliamentary power.

Chartism

Only the presence in Parliament of a large number of working class M.P.'s could guarantee the success of attempts to gain parliamentary power, but working class leaders knew that there was no chance of this while the right to vote was restricted to members of the upper middle class.

The first step was plain enough. The right to vote would have to be given to all classes of society and the wealth qualification which was needed in order to stand as a Parliamentary candidate would have to be abolished. Salaries would also be needed; no worker could be expected to have a private source of income which he could use whilst acting as an M.P., nor was it likely that he would own substantial property.

In 1836 the London Working Men's Association was formed and drew up a six point People's Charter which was published in 1838. The Charter set out the following programme.
1. Universal adult manhood suffrage.
2. Voting to be by secret ballot. (Designed to give people the right to vote for whom they wished without fear of reprisals).
3. Equal electoral districts. (Roughly the same number of voters in each constituency).
4. Abolition of the property qualification for M.P.'s
5. Payment of M.P.'s
6. Annual Parliaments.

It was hoped that, taken together, the six points would give the working classes political power. There was some justification for this hope; the first five of the six points are law today, and the implementation of such reforms undoubtedly helped the rise of the Labour Party.

The Secretary of the London Working Men's Association was William Lovett, an example of one of the best types of Englishman. He was self-educated, well read and possessed great moral courage (he faced prison on behalf of some fellow Chartist on one occasion). Lovett hoped that the aims of the Charter could be achieved peacefully. In 1839 he accepted a suggestion from another reforming organization, the Birmingham Political Union, that a petition should be presented to Parliament demanding the acceptance of the Charter. The petition, signed by over a million people, was duly presented and rejected.

This rejection strengthened the position of a group of Chartist leaders who were opposed to Lovett's peaceful methods and who believed that force would be necessary. Even before the petition had been rejected workingmen in the North had been drilling by torchlight and practising with pikes. A few months after the failure of the petition there was in fact an attempt at an armed uprising in Newport, Monmouthshire. The leader was a local J.P., John Frost, who believed mistakenly that there was to be an uprising in the North. When Frost heard that this rising was not going to take place he

Feargus O'Connor, the fiery leader of Chartism in the North of England.

in a glorious struggle for freedom, and should it please God to spare my life I shall see you soon; but if not, grieve not for me, I shall have fallen in a noble cause. Farewell!

Yours truly,
GEORGE SHELL

A few hours later he was lying dead in Newport.

Chartism did not disappear, but Lovett found it increasingly difficult to exercise control over the wilder elements. In addition the wide divergence of view between the rank and file of the Chartists became more and more obvious.

Feargus O'Connor, an Irishman, then became the leading figure of the movement. He ran a newspaper from Leeds called the *Morning Star* which became a platform for the Chartists. A second petition in 1842 went the way of the first one, and O'Connor became even more dominant. In 1845 he launched a land scheme which looked for a time as if it would be successful. Chartists paid a weekly subscription and the money was used to buy a small holding. The rent from the small holding was then to be used to swell the subscriptions and thus another small holding could be purchased, and so on. It had the ring of 'self help' about it once again, but unfortunately O'Connor did not keep proper accounts and in 1848 the company was found to be bankrupt. Indeed by 1848 so was Chartism. A third and final petition had been planned, and it was arranged that a deputation of Chartists, many from the industrial areas of the

refused to desert his followers and led a hopeless attack on Newport in an attempt to release some Chartists held there. Soldiers were waiting and opened fire on the Chartists gathered in the main square, killing fourteen of them.

One of the Chartists, George Shell, wrote this letter a few hours before the march on Newport.

Pontypool
Sunday Night, Nov. 3, 1839

Dear Parents, I hope this will find you well, as I am myself at this present. I shall this night be engaged

The Chartist meeting at Kennington Common in 1848.

A rather frightened looking citizen being sent on duty to Slaughter's Alley at the time of the Chartist demonstrations of 1848. Middle class 'specials' were used to help keep law and order.

North, should meet on Kennington Common in London. The Government moved in troops and enrolled special constables. Either O'Connor's nerve failed, or common sense prevailed. He told the crowd at Kennington to obey police orders and go home whilst he took the petition in three cabs to the House of Commons. There it was examined and found to have many signatures which were obvious forgeries. It was hardly likely that Queen Victoria, the Duke of Wellington, the Man in the Moon and Mr. Punch would have signed! Chartism collapsed amidst laughter. O'Connor himself ended his days in a lunatic asylum. Sporadic attempts to keep Chartism alive were made in the 1850's but gradually interest shifted to fresh developments, notably a revised interest in the possibility of trade unions.

Looking back one can see that a movement with two men of such conflicting outlooks as Lovett and O'Connor and with such a wide variety of supporters could hardly have hoped to succeed. Moreover, the six points of Chartism were too big a programme to be accomplished at any one time. Many Chartists appear to have been trying to escape from the effects of industrialism, for instance in their land scheme, rather than trying to control it as Owen had hoped.

Each aspect of the industrial changes of the preceding years had produced its discontented class. Skilled London artisans like Lovett felt that they deserved a better place in society. They also felt little in common with Northern handloom weavers facing starvation as the result of the spread of machine weaving. The coal miners of the Newport area were conscious only of the wretched conditions they were forced to work in. What little middle class support there had been for Chartism, mostly from the Birmingham group who wanted a reformed parliament in order to push through currency reforms, had virtually disappeared by the end of 1842.

Friendly Societies

No account of working class self help would be complete without mention of the Friendly Societies.

These were basically clubs designed for mutual self help by means of insurance through regular contributions, against burial costs, sickness and unemployment. They also gave members a chance to meet for a glass of beer or a dinner paid for out of the contributions, thus providing a little touch of light in a drab, if not grim period for the working classes. In this connection it is worth pointing out that these clubs usually drew their members from the better paid workers. Others could not afford the relatively high subscriptions.

During the period of active anti-trade union legislation the Friendly Societies were the only working class organization legally recognized. They were regulated, and on the whole helped by a number of Acts of Parliament from 1793 onwards. From the 1850's a registrar's department was in existence which made a yearly report to the government, and the first registrar, Tidd Pratt, gave valuable help and advice to the Societies.

The important act of 1875 legalized the constitutions' of the bigger Societies and helped them with the preparation of proper insurance (or actuarial information). The scope of insurance offered now included loss of tools, insurance against fire and old age etc.

Some Societies never established themselves on a sound financial footing and collapsed, but the two biggest, the Oddfellows and the Forresters, handled a very large financial turnover. In the 1870's the Oddfellows had a yearly income of £560 000 and their annual sickness and death payments were nearly £400 000.

Although the Societies continued in the twentieth century to make their contribution to working class well-being, the gradual rise of the commercial insurance company (The Prudential appeared in 1848) and the role of the state in the provision of National Insurance have reduced their importance.

QUESTIONS

1. What were the main courses of action open to the working classes in the direction of self-help? Give an example of each.
2. a) Make a chart of the development of Trades Unions up to 1851.
   b) What was the importance of Francis Place?
3. List the six points of the Peoples Charter and find out when five of the six points finally became law.

A mixed train of freight and passengers crosses a viaduct on the Liverpool and Manchester Railway in 1831, see page 62.

SECTION 3

The Great Victorian Age, 1850–1900

On May Day 1851 Queen Victoria, Albert the Prince Consort and their two eldest children rode from Buckingham Palace through the crowded streets of London to open the Great Exhibition in Hyde Park. Extra troops had been moved to the city, and 6000 police were on duty to control the crowds and to deal with the disorders which alarmists said would surely follow the arrival in the capital of thousands of working class families from the north. In the event the precautions were unnecessary. The crowds did not trample the flower beds, throw stones through the windows of the specially constructed Crystal Palace, or move at night through the prosperous West End looting and burning as they went. Instead they behaved with remarkable good humour; walking through the great hall viewing with amazement and pride the thousands of industrial products on show.

In the wealth of items on display and in the calm pride with which they were inspected by the 60 000 visitors who flocked to Hyde Park each day, the Great Exhibition was a symbol of its time. The 'hungry forties', which had been marked by bad harvests, poverty and outbreaks of working class discontent, had already given way to the prosperous fifties. After violent fluctuations trade had settled down, and by 1850 British exports were valued at the unprecedented sum of £71 millions. Northern factories were booming and as unemployment declined wages began to rise. There were still enormous social problems to be solved but for millions of ordinary families in this country life had never been so good. The period of mid-Victorian prosperity had arrived, bringing with it the mood of thrusting self confidence which was the chief characteristic of that age.

By 1867, when the Paris Exhibition was held, some observers noticed that in certain fields Britain was already beginning to fall behind her new industrial rivals like Germany, and in time this challenge was to become really serious. Nevertheless, although her lead was being gradually eaten away, Britain remained the world's most powerful industrial nation during the second half of the nineteenth century, and in Section 3 we shall examine the causes of this economic superiority and see how the life of the nation was affected by it.

10   RAILWAYS AND STEAMSHIPS

The most obvious reason for Britain's commercial superiority in the mid-nineteenth century was the simple fact that industrialization affected this country before similar changes occurred elsewhere. British manufacturers thus gained a lead over their rivals in other countries which was not seriously challenged until the closing years of the century.

Being first in the field was not the only reason for Britain's economic power however. Several other factors contributed to the enormous industrial expansion after 1850 and one of the most important of these was the development of improved methods of transport.

Primitive horse drawn waggonways were in use in the coal mining districts of this country for hundreds of years before the nineteenth century and it was from these simple beginnings that railways as we know them developed. Towards the end of the eighteenth century the number of these tramroads increased, both in the mining areas and in other parts of the country where new waggonways were constructed to act as feeders to the canals. Some of these were improved by the use of cast iron plates in place of the former wooden rails, but they were all very limited. Waggonways

William Hedley's 'Puffing Billy' 1813. It is the oldest locomotive in existence.

Locomotion No 1 which, driven by George Stephenson, drew the first train on the Stockton and Darlington Railway 1825.

Locomotive and railway wagons in use at Hetton Colliery about 1830.

depended on horses for traction and this naturally restricted the size of the loads which could be moved along them.

Early Developments

The answer to this problem was provided by the development of steam railway locomotives, the first of which was built in 1804 by the Cornish engineer Richard Trevithick. This engine ran at the Pen-y-daren Ironworks in South Wales and moved a load of twenty tons at a speed of eight kilometres per hour. The locomotive proved too heavy for the cast iron track, however, and nothing came of the Pen-y-daren experiment. Trevithick built two more engines, one of which he exhibited in London in 1808 but this aroused little interest at the time, and the Cornish inventor abandoned railways and left to seek his fortune in South America.

The idea of steam engines had taken root, however, and various colliery engineers carried on where Trevithick had left off. Blenkinsop built a rack locomotive which ran at the Middleton colliery in Leeds in 1812 and William Hedley constructed his famous *Puffing Billy* at Wylam colliery near Newcastle in 1813. He followed this shortly afterwards with a sister engine called *Wylam Dilly*, and the north east coalfield with its hundreds of short waggonways became the centre of railway development from then on.

George Stephenson, the great railway pioneer.

George Stephenson

George Stephenson, the greatest of the early railway pioneers, was born at Wylam in 1781. He was the son of a poorly paid colliery engine fireman and as one of six children he had to do a variety of jobs as a child before becoming his father's assistant at the age of 14. Stephenson was fascinated by the huge steam engine he worked with and studied it to such good effect that at the age of 17 he was put in charge of a pumping engine. Shortly afterwards he started to catch up on the education he had missed by attending night classes and by the time he was twenty he had laboriously learned to read and write. Further promotion followed as his great practical skill as a mechanic became more widely known, until his determination finally earned him the post he had set his heart on. In 1812 Stephenson was appointed enginewright at the Killingworth colliery not far from his home at a salary of £100 a year.

To rise from cowherd and colliery yard labourer to the position of chief colliery engineer was in itself a remarkable achievement. But far from being the end of Stephenson's career it proved to be only the beginning. In 1814, inspired perhaps by the sight of Hedley's *Puffing Billy*, Stephenson built a colliery locomotive to work the six mile waggonway which connected the Killingworth pit with the Tyne. This engine, which Stephenson called *Blücher* in honour of the famous Prussian general, was as unreliable as all the early locomotives. But Stephenson persevered, and in a series of engines built between 1816 and 1822 he managed to iron out many difficulties. By 1822,

when he built the Hetton Colliery locomotive, which can still be seen in the Railway Museum at York, Stephenson had built up a considerable local reputation as a railway engineer. By this time, too, John Birkinshaw had patented a method of mass producing wrought iron rails in a rolling mill at the Bedlington Ironworks, Blyth, and so railways were ready to take a major step forward.

The Stockton–Darlington Railway

In 1821 Edward Pease, the Quaker mineowner, suggested that a railway should be built to carry coal from the mines round Darlington to the navigable river Tees at Stockton. Stephenson visited Pease and fired the promoter with his own enthusiasm to such an extent that Pease appointed Stephenson as engineer to the line at a salary of £300 a year, and agreed that steam locomotives should be used on what was originally intended to be a horsedrawn railway. Pease also loaned Stephenson enough money to open a locomotive works at Newcastle to be managed by his son Robert.

The Stockton–Darlington Railway took three years to build and by comparison with Stephenson's later works it was a very minor project. It was, nevertheless, the most ambitious scheme which had been tackled up to that time and its opening in 1825 caused great local excitement. Stephenson drove his own '*Locomotion*' at the head of the first train which included one passenger carriage and several trucks carrying the workmen who had helped to build the line. Passengers soon became an important part of the railway's traffic, and this fact gives the Stockton–Darlington Railway its special place in history; it was the world's first passenger-carrying railway.

Robert Stephenson, the equally famous son of a famous father.

The opening of the Stockton and Darlington Railway, 1825.

The Liverpool and Manchester Railway

The cotton merchants of Liverpool and Manchester watched the progress of the Stockton–Darlington Railway with interest. They realized that a similar rail link between their two cities would be of great benefit to the cotton trade, and in 1826 Stephenson was invited to become the engineer on the proposed Liverpool and Manchester Railway.

This was a major undertaking. Almost 64 kilometres separated the two towns and there were considerable engineering problems to be overcome. Stephenson had to float his tracks on a raft of hurdles and brushwood across the treacherous marsh Chat Moss, and extensive excavation was

A model of the locomotive 'Rocket'. The original locomotive was constructed by R. Stephenson & Co to compete for the £500 prize offered by the directors of the Liverpool & Manchester Railway to the makers of the most successful locomotive competing at the Rainhill trials in 1829.

necessary to carry the railway into its Liverpool terminus through the famous Olive Mount cutting. Nevertheless, by 1829 the line was nearly complete and the directors were faced with the task of deciding how it should be worked. Stephenson naturally suggested steam locomotives but some of the directors thought that fixed engines and ropes might prove to be more reliable. To help settle the argument the Rainhill Locomotive Trials were held in October 1829.

Six locomotives were entered for the £500 prize but two of them, which only managed to reach a speed of six miles (9.6 km) an hour, were withdrawn before the competition really began. The remaining four fought it out over the 2.8 kilometre course and the very convincing winner was *Rocket*, designed and built by George and Robert Stephenson. This famous engine, which contained many mechanical improvements, including a tubular boiler, achieved a speed of nearly thirty miles (48 km) per hour and proved very reliable. In view of *Rocket's* success it was decided to use locomotives to work the line throughout most of its length, although fixed engines and cables were used to draw trains up the steep incline from the Liverpool terminus to Edgehill.

Despite the unfortunate accident to Mr. Huskisson, the Liverpool M.P. who was knocked down and fatally injured at the opening ceremony in September 1830, the Liverpool and Manchester Railway was an immediate success. It was soon carrying an average of 1200 passengers a day as well as the bulk of the important cotton traffic between the two cities. Local canal and coach companies found themselves facing financial ruin.

The Liverpool and
Manchester Rly. 1830

Liverpool
Warrington
Manchester
Crewe
The Grand Junction
Railway 1838
Birmingham
London and
Birmingham Rly. 1838
Rugby
London
Bristol
Great Western
Railway 1841

The London Birmingham
Liverpool and Manchester
and Grand Junction Railway
companies amalgamated
in 1846 to form L.N.W.R.

The first main lines 1838 - 41

Development of the Railway System

The opening of the Liverpool and Manchester
Railway marks the real dawn of the 'railway age'.
Its success encouraged other towns to plan rail
links of their own and railway building went
ahead rapidly in the 1830's.

Many of the early lines were short and were
built to serve purely local needs, but before the
end of the decade the first main lines began to
appear. In 1838 Robert Stephenson's London and
Birmingham Railway was completed, and this was
connected to the Liverpool and Manchester
system in the same year, via the Grand Junction
Railway from Birmingham to Warrington. This
created a trunk route from London to industrial
south Lancashire, and a further trunk route was
completed three years later, in 1841, when I. K.
Brunel's seven foot (2.14 m) gauge Great Western
Railway was opened between London and Bristol.

In the 1840's the pace of railway development
increased still further. A great number of new
lines were opened and the first major railway
companies, like the Midland (1844) and the London
and North Western (1846), began to appear as a
result of amalgamations of smaller lines. In 1844
it was possible for George Stephenson to travel
by rail from London to Gateshead, just across
the Tyne, from his home in Newcastle, and by
1850, the year in which Robert Stephenson opened
his Royal Border Bridge across the Tweed, and the
Britannia Tubular Bridge over the Menai Straits,
over 8000 kilometres of railway had been built. It
was possible to travel by rail from London to Glasgow and Edinburgh in Scotland, to Holyhead in
Wales, to the West Country along the broad gauge
Great Western and to any number of points along
the south coast. Almost every town in the country
of any consequence had been reached by the
railways.

The Railway Mania

The money for this amazing railway building
programme was all invested by the public, much
of it during the years of 'railway mania' between
1844 and 1848 when an estimated £233 million
pounds was poured into the railway industry.
This boom in railway share buying and speculation
was similar to the 'canal mania' of the 1790's, but
the amounts of money involved were very much
greater. One of the leading figures in the boom
was George Hudson, the former York draper
who became known in the mid 1840's as the Railway King. He promoted many new lines in the
north of England, played a leading part in the
creation of many large companies by organizing
amalgamations, and at the height of the mania he
handled railway shares worth millions of pounds.
In 1847 however the railway bubble burst. Many
of the companies set up during the mania were
either badly organized or completely bogus, and
when the bottom dropped out of the share market
thousands of pounds were lost. Hudson tried to
hang on to his position of financial power by jug-
gling with the accounts of some of the companies
he controlled, but he was found out. It was also
discovered that he had lined his own pockets
during the time he held positions of trust in public
companies and in 1849 Hudson fell into disgrace.

After Hudson's fall the buying of railway shares
settled down at a less feverish level, but investment was still considerable. Railway companies
were profitable in those days when they had no
road competition, and the 21 760 kilometres of railway which existed in Britain by 1870 were all built
with private money. This is a clear indication of
how wealthy mid-Victorian Britain had become.

Government Control

By the early 1840's the railway network was already
so extensive that, despite its *laissez-faire* outlook,
Parliament felt that some government regulation

George Stephenson's Britannia Bridge across the Menai Straits under construction in 1848.

was necessary. In 1840 the Board of Trade was authorized to inspect all new railways before they opened, and in 1842 the same department was instructed to hold official enquiries into the causes of railway accidents. Gladstone's famous Railway Act of 1844 ordered all railway companies to run at least one train a day on which the fare was to be no more than one penny a mile, and so rail travel was brought within the reach of the poor. The same act contained a clause which gave the state the right to take over the railways after 21 years, but this option was not taken up until the present century.

In 1846 Parliament intervened to settle the 'battle of the gauges' by ordering that all railways built in the future, with the exception of those

Important top-hatted guests, including Mr. Gladstone, about to take the first journey on the new London underground railway in 1863.

lines associated with the Great Western, should have a gauge of four feet, eight and a half inches (1.44 m). This was a sensible move to ease the interchange of traffic between the lines of different companies, but Brunel was disgusted that 'Stephenson's horse and cart gauge' had been chosen in preference to his own. In time Parliament extended its control over many other railway matters and fixed maximum fares and freight rates in the public interest, but no attempt was made to take the railways out of private hands until the present century.

The Effects of Railways

The coming of the railways was of enormous importance. They provided industry with a means of transport far superior to anything which had existed before and encouraged tremendous economic growth. They were also a valuable new source of employment, and in time the manufacture of railway equipment became established as an important industry in its own right in railway towns like Crewe, Darlington and Swindon.

By encouraging people to travel the railways brought about a minor social revolution. New suburban areas began to grow on the outskirts of our large towns, easing the problem of urban overcrowding, and seaside holiday resorts sprang up catering for day trippers and workers on their annual week's holiday. The railways created Blackpool just as surely as they created Crewe.

The spread of railways abroad (many of which were built by British engineers) had even more remarkable results. They played a large part in the industrialization of Western Europe and by opening up the great wheatlands of the United States and Canada they provided food for the rapidly growing town populations of the industrial nations. In India, South America, Africa and the Far East railways brought progress to some of the remotest areas of the world, and Professor Trevelyan was not exaggerating when he called railways 'England's gift to the world'.

STEAMSHIPS

Important as the new rail links were, they were not the only development in transport which aided Britain's commercial expansion in the midnineteenth century. The same years which saw the development of railways also saw the emergence of the steamship.

Early Developments

The first successful steamship in this country was the *Charlotte Dundas* which sailed on the Forth Clyde Canal in 1802 towing two 70 ton barges. Her designer was the Scottish engineer William Symington who had patented the marine engine in 1786. Symington's work aroused the interest of Robert Fulton, an American who was living in England at the time, and he visited Symington in order to study his ideas. After this meeting Fulton returned to America with two engines he had ordered from the firm of Boulton and Watt, in order to continue his experiments there. In 1807 he successfully launched *Clermont* on the Hudson River, thus beginning the story of the development of the steamship in the United States. Back in Britain another Scottish engineer named Henry Bell had been carrying out

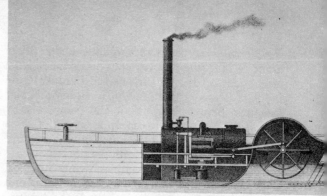

The machinery of the 'Charlotte Dundas'.

experiments of his own quite independently of Symington, and in 1812 his *Comet* was successfully tried out on the Forth-Clyde Canal. This small vessel, which later ventured out along the coast as far as Leith, was the most successful of the early steamships and was used for regular passenger services on the Clyde. Similar steam ferry services were operating on the Mersey and Thames soon after, and in 1816 steam sailings across the Irish Sea began between Holyhead and Dublin, and Greenock and Belfast. In 1818 the cross-Channel steamer service between Dover and Calais was opened and by 1829 the steamship was considered reliable enough to start carrying the mails.

By Steam Across the Atlantic

Like all new inventions the steamship aroused a tremendous amount of ridicule and hostility and much of this was reserved for those people who suggested that regular steam sailings across the Atlantic were possible. The American vessel *Savannah* made a crossing in 1819 with some assistance from her engines but even after the Canadian ship

William Symington's 'Charlotte Dundas'.

Royal William crossed the Atlantic under steam alone in 1833 (the first vessel to do so) the ridicule continued. An Irish doctor named Lardner wrote in 1836 'it was just as fanciful to attempt regular crossings between Liverpool and New York by steamship, as it was to set up a service of ships between Liverpool and the moon' and there were many people who agreed with the doctor's views. Events were soon to prove them wrong however. The *Sirius*, Brunel's *Great Western* and a second vessel named *Royal William* all made the Atlantic crossing successfully in 1838. The *Great Western* took only thirteen and a half days to complete the journey and the government now began to take notice. In 1839 they put up the contract to carry the Atlantic mails to tender and in 1840 Samuel Cunard, the Canadian Shipowner who won the contract, began a regular steam service from Liverpool to Halifax, Nova Scotia and later to New York. The steamship had conquered one of the cruellest of all the great oceans.

Progress in Steamship Design

By 1840 steamships had proved themselves to be safe and reliable, but, for all that, steam only replaced sail very slowly. The engines and the enormous amounts of coal which early steamships carried, cut down the amount of cargo space so drastically that sailing ships remained more economic for many years. In time, however, a number of technical developments tipped the balance in favour of steam.

In 1843 Brunel built the *Great Britain*, a revolutionary vessel incorporating the recently developed screw propeller and a hull made entirely of iron. This gave the ship immense strength, a point which was brought home forcefully in 1846 when the *Great Britain* ran aground off the Irish coast and was successfully refloated after eleven months of being battered by heavy seas. From the 1840's onwards iron, and later steel, became the chief materials used in shipbuilding and this encouraged the use of heavier and more powerful engines which, coupled with the screw propeller, gave greater speeds. In 1854 John Elder, a Clydeside shipbuilder, developed the compound steam engine which, by using the same steam several times over in different sized cylinders, led to great economies in fuel. This was a major step forward and allowed steamers to become more economic for cargo carrying purposes.

The Great Eastern

By the late 1850's steam ships were becoming bigger and more powerful and were in use on all the oceans of the world. It was at this stage that Brunel designed one of the most remarkable of the all, the *Great Eastern*. This giant vessel, which was 680 feet (207 m) long and weighed 3800 tons, had one propellor, two paddles, five funnels and six masts to carry additional sails. She was designed to carry 4000 passengers. Unfortunately, like so many of Brunel's ideas, she was years ahead of her time and was a colossal commercial failure. An explosion on her maiden voyage which killed six men gave the *Great Eastern* the reputation of being an unlucky ship, and passengers were not anxious to sail in her. She did her best service in 1866 when

A rare photograph of Brunel's 'Great Eastern' taken about 1860.

This picture gives a good idea of the size of the 'Great Eastern'. Note the enormous paddle wheel.

Parson's 'Turbinia' at speed.

she was used to lay the Atlantic telegraph cable. Then she was bought by a circus proprietor and moored alongside Liverpool landing stage as a floating fairground. Even in this role the *Great Eastern* did not make money, and she was finally sold to a scrap merchant and towed to New Ferry in Cheshire to be broken up. This last owner was the only one to make money out of her.

The financial and technical problems of building and launching *Great Eastern* were the chief cause of Brunel's death. In 1859 he fell gravely ill and a few days after being drawn across his last great masterpiece, the Saltash railway bridge, on a contractors waggon because he was too ill to walk, Brunel died. 1859 was also the year in which his great friend and rival Robert Stephenson died.

The Triumph of Steam

The failure of the *Great Eastern* did not affect the future of steamships. The opening, in 1869, of the Suez Canal, which could only be used by steamers, gave them a virtual monopoly of trade with the Far East and further technical developments increased their efficiency. A notable achievement in this direction was the development of the steam turbine by Sir Charles Parsons of Newcastle in 1884. He fitted one of these engines into the *Turbinia* in 1894 and demonstrated that the new engine had tremendous power. Over the next twenty years it came into widespread use.

By 1913 steam had triumphed. A last fight was put up in the 60's and 70's by beautiful clipper ships like the *Cutty Sark*, but in 1913 the tonnage of sailing vessels in the British merchant fleet had dwindled from 4 000 000 tons in 1873 to a mere 800 000 tons. In the same years steam tonnage had risen from 1 700 000 to a staggering 11 300 000 tons. When the First World War broke out in 1914 Britain had far and away the biggest merchant navy in the world, with almost half the total world tonnage of merchant ships. Appropriately enough many of these vessels had been built in the busy shipyards along the Clyde, the river which was the cradle of the steamship.

QUESTIONS

1. Write an account of the career of George Stephenson.
2. What was the 'Railway Mania'?
3. What were the main effects of the coming of the railways?
4. Describe in your own words the development of steamships in the nineteenth century.

11 FREE TRADE AND THE CORN LAWS

The changes in agriculture and industry described in earlier chapters were to have far reaching effects on Britain's trading policies in the nineteenth century.

For hundreds of years, Britain, in common with other nations, had concentrated on protecting her industries and agriculture from overseas competition by means of a system of import and export duties rather than by allowing a free movement of goods and raw materials in and out of the country. Goods entering Britain had to pay an import duty so that they would not challenge or undermine the prices of the home products. Exports, including raw materials, carried heavy duties, the argument behind such measures being that they would make Britain self supporting. In addition, Parliament had passed Navigation Acts which reinforced the system by forbidding the export of British goods other than in British ships and which prohibited the emigration of skilled workers and the export of machinery. The idea behind all this legislation was to make Britain financially strong through being self reliant.

In the absence of income tax these duties were an important source of revenue for the government and were also to be found on items which did not threaten any home based industry, items such as tea and brandy. It was a golden age for the smuggler running his cargoes to some quiet spot on the coasts of Britain and finding a ready market for goods which had not paid a tax to His Majesty.

But it could also be a hazardous life for him and for the preventive officers of the Customs and Excise, and makes an interesting comparison with the present day smuggling of human beings across the English Channel in order to get round the Immigration Laws.

In 1820 a writer in the Edinburgh Review summed up the feelings of the British people:

'Taxes upon every article which enters the mouth, or covers the back, or is placed under the foot . . . taxes on the sauce which pampers man's appetite, that restores him to health—on the ermine which decorates the judge, and rope which hangs the criminal—on the poor man's salt and the rich man's spice—on the brass nails of the coffin, and the ribands of the bride . . . and the dying Englishman pouring his medicine which has paid seven per cent, into a spoon that has paid fifteen per cent—flings himself back upon his chintz bed which has paid twenty two per cent—makes his will on an eight pound stamp, and expires in the arms of an apothecary who has paid a licence of £100 for the privilege of putting him to death.'

This vast network of duties had become so complicated over the years that the income from them was sometimes swallowed up by the cost of collection. As C. R. Fay, the historian, said 'the collection of the excise duties needed a great army of excise men . . . at the head of the army were the Collectors, 55 in all in 1835; under them the County Supervisors, under them the Ride Officers for country districts, the Footwalk Officers for towns, the Special London Officers for London'.

Such a system needed overhauling if only on grounds of economy. But this in itself would probably not have been a sufficient cause for the sweeping changes in Britain's methods of trade which came about in the first half of the nineteenth

A smuggler pursued by a customs man. The cartoonist Cruikshank's view of the smuggling trade.

Smugglers in the eighteenth century bringing an illegal cargo ashore. A romantic view of the business.

century. A more powerful reason lay in the increasing pressure for new markets arising out of our rapidly increasing output of factory produced goods. The growing middle class of merchants and factory owners felt that they no longer needed 'protection' from foreign rivals. They knew that they could outprice any competitor as a result of Britain's great lead in the use of machinery. They wanted low export duties for their products and they also wanted low import duties so that other countries would find it easier to trade with Britain. The factory owners knew that our cheaply made textiles would be able to dominate European markets.

It took a long time for our manufacturers to achieve all that they wanted for they faced the unwavering hostility of one particular group of men: the landowners who depended on protection to safeguard British farming from the danger, as they saw it, of cheap foreign corn.

Thus the freeing of trade from restrictive duties was an inevitable follow-on from the development of machinery and the factory system. Before the mechanization of the cotton industry, Lancastrians had been in favour of the protection provided by import taxes without which the Lancashire cottons could not possibly have faced the competition of Indian textiles. With the security of having more advanced machinery than the rest of the world, which had yet to experience the Industrial Revolution, a very different attitude was adopted. In 1813 when the East India Company's monopoly of trade with India was finally abolished, the textile towns were petitioning Parliament to open up trade with India. 'Freedom of commerce is one of the birth-rights of Britons', they said. It apparently had not been so a few decades earlier.

The Theory of Free Trade

What has been outlined above was the practical side of the matter. There was also the development of the theory of free trade and the advantages to be gained from such a step. The most important theorist was a Scotsman, Adam Smith, born in Kircaldy, educated at Glasgow and Oxford Universities (he made some nasty remarks about the Oxford of the period) and returned to Glasgow as a professor. In 1776 came his famous book 'An Inquiry into the Nature and Causes of the Wealth of Nations'. In it he attacked the whole system of protection—and pointed out that when there was free trade, buyers and sellers could get rid of their surplus stocks and buy what they needed. He claimed that cramping government regulations, many of which survived from the days of Elizabeth I, restricting movement of people from one parish to another, governing hours of work and standards of workmanship should be abolished. In their place should be put the idea of self interest, what he called

'The natural effort of every individual to better his own conditions, ... is ... not only capable of carrying the society to wealth and prosperity, but of surmounting a hundred impertinent obstructions'.

It was this self interest that was cramped by internal regulations and external taxes. Free it and the individual enterprise of man to enrich himself would enrich the nation. In other words this is the

69

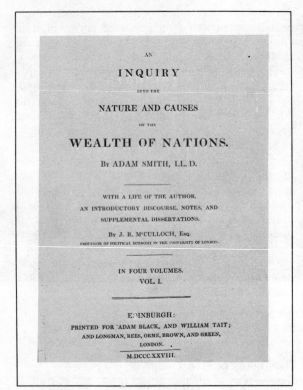

Title page of Adam Smith's 'Wealth of Nations'.

doctrine of *laissez-faire* mentioned in Chapter 7. Unfortunately it could also lead to opposition to Factory Acts, the proper planning of towns and a veto on State help for the poor arising from the view that it was not for a government to interfere in such matters.

Steps to Free Trade

The first man to tackle the maze of customs duties was William Pitt, Prime Minister of Britain after the disastrous war in which we lost our American colonies. Pitt's real concern was to see Britain regain her financial strength after this war, and as a consequence he concentrated on the inefficiency of the system rather than attempting sweeping changes. In any case the concerted power of the factory owners lay in the future, although he did listen to the suggestions of individual middle class manufacturers such as Boulton and Wedgewood, and he had read Adam Smith. In 1792 he mentioned 'the writings of an author of our times . . . whose extensive knowledge . . . will furnish the best solution to every question connected with the history of commerce'.

What Pitt aimed to do was to weaken the smuggler by replacing some of the customs duties paid at ports of entry by a tax paid when the commodities were actually sold to the consumer. Pitt also made use of an idea put forward by Adam Smith, that of the reciprocal treaty. In this type of treaty two countries agree to lower certain duties on each other's imports and exports. In 1786, Pitt concluded such a treaty with France whereby our manufactures were allowed into France at a reduced customs rate in return for French wines and spirits receiving similar-favourable treatment from Britain.

Another important step taken by Pitt was forced upon him by war costs once again, for in 1793 Britain and France became locked in the French revolutionary and Napoleonic wars which continued almost uninterrupted for over twenty years. The immense debts run up by Britain led Pitt to impose an income tax. It was levied at a standard rate of 10% (10p in the £), with allowance for children and insurance, amid a howl of disapproval. It helped to finance the war and although it was discontinued at the end of the war with France its example remained as an attractive alternative to raising revenue from customs duties.

The Work of Huskisson

Peace came in 1815 and in the 1820's William Huskisson, who was President of the Board of Trade from 1823–1827, carried out a number of reductions in customs duties. Huskisson was one of the M.P.'s for Liverpool during this period and was thus sympathetic to the increasing clamour for the freeing of trade that was coming from the merchants and manufacturers of the industrial North of England. It was also a fairly prosperous time for the country as a whole and Huskisson was able to carry out changes in three main fields.

He reduced import duties. An upper limit of 30% was set on raw materials and semi finished goods. Silk for instance paid this duty when it came into Britain. Many items, however, paid a much lower rate. Cotton carried a 10% rate only, the point being that our silk industry was felt to need more protection than our cotton industry.

Huskisson also reduced or abolished a number of the excise duties (payable on purchase) on such things as salt, starch and sweets. The excise duty on wine went in 1825. Finally Huskisson reformed the navigation laws making it easier for merchants to use foreign ships to carry cargoes to England.

Huskisson was only altering duties, he was not changing a system. Protective import duties still remained and attractive European markets remained closed to Britain because of this.

Sir Robert Peel.

Peel

It was Sir Robert Peel, during his period as Prime Minister from 1841–1846, who really brought about a decisive change in the system. Peel's idea was simple. Trade would be freed of restriction, would prosper and thus bring prosperity to the country. Necessary government revenue would come from an income tax which would bridge the gap in revenue that Peel anticipated until his measures began to work.

In his budget of 1842 and 1845 Peel slashed import duties (Peel although not Chancellor of the Exchequer took responsibility for these budgets). In 1842 raw material paid 5%, semi-manufactured goods paid 12% and fully manufactured goods carried 20%, a reduction of 10% on Huskisson's top level. In 1843 it became possible to freely export machinery. In 1844 export and import duties on raw wool were abolished. Then in 1845 he picked up the threads of his 1842 budget. Most of the 5% raw material duties were abolished and the fully manufactured rate was lowered to 10%.

Peel felt able to do this because of his success in bridging the gap in government revenue. He had put on income tax as a temporary measure in 1842 at 7d. (3p) in the pound and the money from it and a duty on coal had more than compensated for the drop in customs revenue. Peel decided to continue income tax in 1845 still hoping that it would be possible to drop it once the revenue had made up temporary losses. Alas it was not to be. Other reasons compelled later ministers to keep the tax and in our day we would gladly settle for 3p as a standard rate of 'the very wickedest and most vexatious of taxes which the ingenuity of man could devise'.

Peel's last act was to break the greatest single prohibitive tax, that on imported corn which he abolished in 1846. The act also broke him, as we shall see below.

The finishing touches to the movement towards free trade came from Gladstone in 1853 and 1860. By 1860 all duties on manufactures had gone (no 10% or 20% now). In 1853 and in 1861 Gladstone abolished excise duties on soap and paper, which, he said, were taxes on cleanliness and knowledge. The last traces of the navigation laws had disappeared by 1851. Preferential treatment (i.e. lower taxes) for the British Empire disappeared automatically in this general abolition. It was a case of a fair field and no favour, and so it remained until British industry and its techniques were overtaken by foreign competitors and then the cry for protection was heard again, this time protection from more efficient and up to date foreign competition.

The Abolition of the Corn Laws: the Victory of the Industrialist over the Landowner

This aspect of the movement towards free trade is so important that it deserves a separate section. The abolition of the Corn Laws finished the career of a great Prime Minister, broke up a great political party and marked the relatively greater importance of industry as compared to agriculture by the middle of the nineteenth century in Britain.

The Corn Law which caused the trouble had been passed in 1815. It said simply that until the price of English grown corn reached £4 a quarter there was to be a total ban on the import of foreign corn. Only when the price of £4 was reached would foreign corn be admitted to Britain. This was nothing more than a move by a Parliament packed with landlords to protect their own interests and those of their tenants. If the harvest was good in Britain then the price of corn would be low. Indeed in some years it lay around the £2.50 per quarter level. In this case there was no foreign competition to worry about. If the home harvest was bad then the English farmer got his high price in any case. This situation may have benefitted the farmers, although there is no sign that English agriculture flourished behind the protective screen, but it did not benefit merchants, who sometimes imported corn when English corn stood at the required rate of £4 only to find the home price drop and their consignments left to rot in warehouses. Liverpool merchants in particular pressed Huskisson on this point.

Thus in the 1820's the government found that demands were being made for change in a law which was obviously aimed to benefit one small but extremely powerful and wealthy section of the community. It introduced a sliding scale in 1828 which allowed the importation of foreign corn at a rate of duty which decreased as the price of English corn rose.

This again was only tampering with the law. In the 1830's the manufacturers began to build up their opposition to the law until it reached such a pitch that in 1839 the Anti-Corn Law League was formed.

The Anti-Corn Law League

This was an organization of middle class manufacturers whose aim was to abolish the hated law. Until it went they could see no hope of trading with countries whose only means of paying for our manufactured exports was by selling corn to Britain, for if they could not sell corn then they either did without our manufactures or, worse, they began to develop their own. The Free Traders were able to combine self interest and internationalism. 'Let each country produce what it best can. We will supply the world with manufactured goods, they will send us food'. The League was also able to claim righteously to be campaigning for cheaper bread and thus cut the cost of living of the workers. The protectionist landlords who in fact had an Anti-Anti-Corn Law organization were not slow to point out that if the factory owners paid better wages to their workpeople there would be no need to clamour about cheaper bread.

The League faced a stiff fight for the protectionists were well entrenched in parliament. They were often in a position to make it impossible for the League to hold meetings in some county areas by forbidding their tenants to attend, or by refusing permission to use the local meeting rooms.

However, the League had more powerful weapons. In John Bright and Richard Cobden they had two of the best middle class leaders in the nineteenth century. Both men were able to convince their public meeting audiences that their motives were not selfish; that their concern was for cheap bread and general world peace brought about by free trade between one nation and another. They cleverly attacked the landlords making out that wars were caused by aristocrats 'the sooner the power in this country is transferred from the landed oligarchy (the upper class aristocratic land-owners) which has so misused it; and is placed absolutely—mind I say absolutely—in the hands of the intelligent middle and industrious classes, the better for the condition and destinies of this country'. So spoke Cobden.

The League did not hesitate to label their opponents as 'foot-pad aristocrats', 'bread-stealers', 'Chaw bacon, bull frog and clod pate farmers'. It used the new railways and penny post to spread its ideas, and unlike the workers who were struggling with their Chartist organization at the same period, the League had money. The industrialists poured in their subscriptions—£50 000 in 1843, £80 000 in 1844. The long purses of the factory owners were used to the full yet the repeal of the Corn Laws in 1846 came as a result of events in Ireland.

In 1845 the Irish potato crop failed. As the Irish began to die in their thousands owing to their

Cobden addressing a meeting of the Anti-Corn Law League.

absolute dependence on the potato for food, it became clear that massive corn imports were needed. Yet these could not be brought in unless the Corn Law was repealed. The Prime Minister, Peel, leader of the Tory party which was largely in favour of keeping the law, had privately made up his mind that the law should go. But his own party might not support him. Many great landowners were in its ranks, and after all it was Ireland and not England that was starving, and this was an age that saw Queen Victoria give £3 to the starving Irish and £50 to the R.S.P.C.A. Peel put people first, and with the support of part of his own party and the other main party, the Whigs, he was able to repeal the law. But the measure split the Tory party and led to Peel being turned out of office on the same day as he repealed the Corn Law by a combination of Whigs and protectionist Tories.

The middle class had not only gained another step on the road to free trade, they had won a decisive victory on behalf of the new industrial England over the older agricultural England. As for Ireland repeal came too late to save hundreds of thousands of the wretched inhabitants of that country from dying of starvation. Even when supplies of maize did reach Ireland it was used in such a way that the term 'Peel's brimstone' was applied to it.

QUESTIONS

1. Explain the following terms:
   a) 'Protection'.
   b) Navigation Laws.
   c) Monopoly.
   d) Free Trade.
2. Explain what the attitude of the manufacturer was to the question of free trade. What were the views of many of the landowners?
3. What contribution towards the freeing of trade did the following men make:
   a) William Pitt.
   b) Adam Smith.
   c) Huskisson.
   d) Peel.
   e) Gladstone.
4. What were the aims and methods of the anti-Corn Law League?

Starving Irish peasants asking for food at a workhouse during the potato famine in 1846.

12 INDUSTRY AND AGRICULTURE 1850–1900

Between 1850 and 1900 Britain became an industrial nation. In 1851 the population, numbering about 20 millions, was divided equally between town and country. By 1900, when the population was 37 millions, 75% of the people were living in towns, and only 25% in the country. Industry and the profits of exported manufactured goods had become the nation's chief way of earning its living.

Industrial Progress

The growth of population in the towns was directly associated with the enormous expansion of British industry in the second half of the nineteenth century. The full effects of railway building and the government's policy of free trade enabled manufacturers to satisfy the demands of a growing world market, and every major British industry increased its output after 1850. Coal production for example, which stood at 45 million tons a year in the mid-1840's, rose to 90 million tons a year by 1860 and to 228 million tons by 1900. Iron showed a similar rapid growth from 3 million tons a year in 1855 to 6 million tons in 1875, while textiles soared ahead achieving remarkable export figures. In 1845 849 million yards of cotton piece goods had been exported from Britain, a figure which jumped to 2000 million yards in 1860 and to over 5000 million in 1900. As a result, textiles remained throughout this period the country's most important single export commodity. Rapid advances were also made in shipbuilding, glass, and pottery manufacture and indeed in all Britain's old established industries which had grown up as a result of the Industrial Revolution.

New Industries

The period from 1850 to 1900 also saw the development of a large number of new industries, many of them producing consumer goods for which there was an expanding market owing to the rising standards of living in this country. The boot and shoe industry, centred on Northampton, grew rapidly following the introduction of J. M. Singer's sewing machine from the United States, and manufacturers of ready-made clothing established themselves in a big way for the same reason. Soap firms like Levers, manufacturers of biscuits like

Women workers marking boxes for Sunlight soap at the Lever Brother's factory in the 1890's.

Huntley and Palmers, and chocolate campanies such as Frys and Cadburys also expanded at this time, with brand names such as Sunlight and Bourneville becoming household words. Changes in social habits, for example the craze for cycling in the 1880's and 1890's, also promoted new industries and Coventry and Birmingham became the centres of the bicycle manufacturing industry. This in turn led to the growth of a thriving British rubber industry following the invention of the pneumatic tyre by J. B. Dunlop, a Belfast veterinary surgeon in 1888. Other new industries appeared as a result of the advances made in science in the late nineteenth century, for example the manufacture of artificial silk, ferro-concrete and electrical goods. But most noteworthy of all was the remarkable growth of the steel industry.

The Röver Safety Bicycle 1885. The ancestor of all modern bicycles.

The Steel Industry

Steel is iron which contains a known quantity of carbon (between .3 and 1.5%), and it has special qualities which make it suitable for the manufacture of edge tools and items which require a metal which is both strong and flexible, for instance watch springs. Nowadays steel is used for a variety of purposes and is the most common everyday metal but in 1850 this was not so. Production of steel then stood at only 40 000 tons a year and, since it was very expensive, its use was confined to cutlery, machine tools and certain other high quality products.

Steel was expensive because it was very difficult to make. Traditionally it had been produced by the cementation process in which bars of wrought iron containing very little carbon were placed in close contact with charcoal and heated and reheated in a sealed furnace. Gradually some of the carbon in the charcoal entered the iron and steel was produced. This was a very hit and miss method, and in 1740 Benjamin Huntsman, a Sheffield clockmaker who wanted good steel for his clock springs, developed an improved means of production. He melted bars of iron in fire clay containers called crucibles at very high temperatures. The carbon in the iron was burnt away leaving pure molten iron to which Huntsman added the correct amount of carbon to produce very good quality steel. Crucible steel was expensive, however, because it could only be produced in small quantities, and so, unlike the iron industry, which as we saw in Chapter 4 made rapid strides in the eighteenth century, the steel industry remained small.

The technical revolution which created the modern steel industry began in 1856 with the introduction of the Bessemer converter. This was a large cylindrical vessel which could hold several tons of molten pig iron (iron with a high carbon content), and through which a blast of air could be forced. The air created sufficient heat inside the converter to burn away all the carbon, leaving pure molten iron. To this the required amount of carbon was added to produce steel. Bessemer's steel was not of the same quality as crucible steel and the Sheffield steel masters scoffed at his product when he established a works there to manufacture it. For some purposes, however, his steel was ideal, and ship and railway builders soon became his eager customers. After fourteen years Bessemer was able to sell his works for twenty-four times their original cost and he earned over £1 000 000 in royalties from other firms who copied his process.

Another important development in the steel industry came in 1866 when William Siemens, a naturalized Briton of German birth, invented the open hearth process. By using a mixture of coal gas and air for the blast, and a complicated regenerative furnace to pre-heat the air and create very high temperatures, Siemens was able to manufacture steel without the use of the bell shaped converter; hence the name open hearth. Thus by 1870 there were two rival methods available for mass producing steel and the industry developed rapidly.

Both the Bessemer and the open hearth processes suffered from a serious drawback. They could not use iron ores which contained phosphorus, and since most British ore does contain phosphorus much of the iron used to manufacture steel in the 1860's and 1870's was imported from Sweden and other places abroad. The answer to this particular problem was provided in 1878 by a third English inventor: Sydney Gilchrist-Thomas,

A Bessemer converter in use in the giant Krupp Steelworks at Essen in Germany in the late 19th. century.

Thomas process was not Britain but Germany. After Bismarck's successful war against France in 1870 he seized the rich iron area of Lorraine where the ores contained a high percentage of phosphorus. Using these ores and the abundant coal from the Ruhr, the richest coalfield in Europe, Germany was able to built up a massive steel industry; a leading part being played by the giant Krupp arms firm. In America, too, the various steel making processes developed in this country were put to good use and steel output in the United States passed that of Britain in 1890. Six years later German steel production was also greater than ours, and since steel was becoming the basis of industrial power this was a sign of the times. In fact from about 1875 onwards Britain's unique position as the 'workshop of the world' was being challenged by new industrial rivals.

This foreign competition was to be expected. Britain had built up her economic power by exploiting her reserves of coal and iron in the late eighteenth and early nineteenth centuries, but her resources of both raw materials and manpower were not as great as those of Germany and the United States. When these two nations embarked on a policy of rapid industrialization and protected

Tapping an open-hearth furnace in a Teeside steel works at the present day.

a London chemist. Working with his cousin P.C. Gilchrist, Thomas found that by lining a converter with a basic material, such as limestone or dolomite, it was possible to eliminate the phosphorus from the iron. He demonstrated his technique in Middlesbrough in April 1879 at the works of the firm of Bolckow and Vaughan (now the giant Dorman Long steelworks which is part of the British Steel Corporation) and the demonstration was an outstanding success. A local journalist noted that soon afterwards the town was filled with steelmen from Belgium, France, Germany, Austria and the United States, all anxious to know more about the technique. For Middlesbrough, with the large Cleveland iron field on its doorstep, the Gilchrist-Thomas process was the beginning of a rapid era of progress, and for the British steel industry generally it was a major breakthrough. Steel could now be produced in large quantities from ore mined in this country, and the table shown here indicates the strides made by the industry.

The Challenge to Britain's Economic Power

The nation which benefited most from the Gilchrist-

their industries with high customs barriers, Britain was bound to be affected. As a result of our enormous industrial lead and our command of world-wide markets the threat was more in the future than at the time, and as we have seen British industry continued to grow throughout the last half of the nineteenth century. But it did not grow as fast as that of our chief rivals, and it is significant that after over a hundred years of being in the forefront of every major technical advance, Britain played a very small part in the development of the motor car. By 1900 this country was nearing the end of its economic and industrial heyday.

The Decline of Agriculture

Foreign competition in the mid seventies was not only confined to industry. Agriculture also suffered, and here the effects were more sudden and much more serious.

The repeal of the Corn Laws in 1846 (see page 71) did not bring ruin to British farms as many had predicted, in fact the effect was quite the reverse. Free trade encouraged industry and the growth of towns, and gave to the farmers an expanding and increasingly prosperous market. The railways provided a speedy and reliable means of transporting farm produce into the towns, and farming

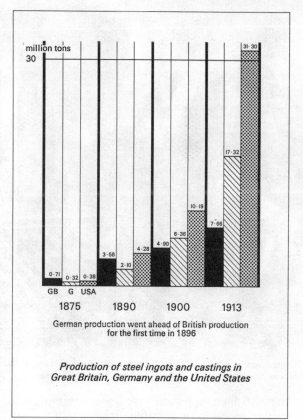

million tons
30

	GB	G	USA						
1875	0·71	0·32	0·38						
1890				3·58	2·10	4·28			
1900							4·90	6·36	10·19
1913							7·66	17·32	31·30

German production went ahead of British production
for the first time in 1896

*Production of steel ingots and castings in
Great Britain, Germany and the United States*

*The Krupp stand at the 1902 exhibition in Dusseldorf, Germany.
Armaments like these made the German army the best equipped in
the world.*

Steam ploughing about 1850. Note how the engine remains in one position and draws the plough across the field on a strong cable. The Hunt in the background are obviously unconcerned by progress.

began to flourish. Farming methods were improved by the adoption of scientific drainage, improved fertilizers and cattle feed, and the more widespread use of steam power, and so output rose. Most farmers concentrated on producing wheat and beef, the commodities for which there was the greatest demand, and, as a result of the new techniques and the fact that prices were high, profits were good. For the countryman with land of his own, or land that he had rented, life had never been so good. Not much of the new prosperity filtered down to the ordinary farm worker, but even he was sure of a job, and so for the countryside generally this was a golden age.

The end came suddenly. The rapid growth of railways in this country helped the farmer, but their rapid growth in the United States helped to ruin him. The opening up of the prairies by the American railroads in the 1870's brought millions of acres of cornland into competition with the British farms. Reaped by steam harvesters and brought to Britain in steamshops, American wheat could undersell British wheat to such an extent that the prices of home grown grain began to tumble. Farmers who sold their harvests in 1877 for fifty-six shillings and six pence (£2.82½) a quarter could only get thirty-one shillings (£1.55) a quarter for their wheat in 1886. This competition, coupled with a series of bad harvests, particularly that of 1879, the wettest year

on record, ruined many British farmers. Some went bankrupt altogether, while others attempted to ride out the storm by turning away from wheat growing to other branches of agriculture. The acreage under wheat in this country fell dramatically from over 3½ million acres in 1874 to only just over half that figure in 1900.

On top of this disaster to wheat farming came a further blow which affected livestock farmers. This was the introduction of refrigeration. In 1880 the steamship *Dunedin* docked at London with a cargo of frozen New Zealand meat, and from that time onwards beef and mutton producers in this country found themselves in competition with Australian and New Zealand lamb and beef from the Argentine. In addition, refrigeration allowed the importation of foreign butter and cheese and thus increased competition in dairy farming at a time when many farmers were turning to this branch of agriculture as a way out of their difficulties.

It took farming many years to recover from these twin blows. Wheat prices continued to fall until they reached rock bottom in 1894 at twenty-two shillings (£1.10) a quarter, and the population of the farming districts dwindled as more and more people left the country to find work in the towns. Those who remained behind faced the difficult task of adapting to the new circumstances. It was obviously no longer profitable to concentrate on the production of wheat and beef and so farming began to change. By 1914 market gardening had become a flourishing industry in country areas near to the big cities, and in other regions farmers had recovered by concentrating on quality as opposed to quantity; producing first class livestock, for example, which could compete with imported meat. Since that time, the two World Wars, the greater use of tractors and other forms of farm machinery and the increased application of science to agriculture have all stimulated a revival in farming. Today farming is a prosperous industry and the agricultural slump of the period 1875 to 1914 is very much a thing of the past. Nevertheless, for those farmers who lived through them, the lean years at the end of the last century were a time of extreme difficulty, and they reminded the nation as a whole that Britain's prosperity was not automatic and would not necessarily last forever.

Conclusion

In the years between 1850 and 1900 Britain went through an economic revolution. For twenty-five years, from 1850 to 1875, both industry and agriculture flourished and the nation enjoyed a position of undisputed economic power. After 1875 the effects of foreign competition began to be felt. Agriculture suffered first and took many years to recover. The blow to industry was less immediately apparent because it was cushioned by our enormous industrial lead, but it was a sign that the future was going to be difficult. It would be true to say that the economic problems which still plague Britain in the second half of the twentieth century first became apparent in the second half of the nineteenth.

QUESTIONS

1. Describe the progress made by Britain's older industries in the late nineteenth century.
2. Why did so many new industries grow up after 1850?
3. What contributions did Bessemer, Siemens and Gilchrist-Thomas make to the progress of the steel industry?
4. Which two countries challenged Britain's economic supremacy in the late nineteenth century? What advantages did they have over Britain?
5. What caused the decline in British farming after 1875? How serious was their decline?

13   REFORM AND THE PEOPLE

One of the leaders of the Chartist movement writing in 1885, many years after its collapse, deplored the change in attitude of the working men he met. They seemed to him to have lost their burning desire for radical change. To him England seemed to have gone 'soft'. This was hardly so by our standards, for we would think that life then was harsh and bitter, but it *was* true that a variety of reforms had made life more bearable for many working class men and women.

To some extent the working classes themselves had contributed to this improvement. The struggle for the People's Charter outlined in Chapter 9 had not interested all working class leaders. Some still regarded trade union activity as the best means of improving their lot. For instance the coal miners

formed an association in the 1840's, and used legal help in fighting their employers. It became noticeable that there was less talk of revolution in the T.U. Movement, and a greater concentration on working within the existing framework of society rather than attempting to overturn it.

The New Model Unionism

In 1851 the Amalgamated Society of Engineers was formed, and the way in which it was organized became a model for the trade union activity of the period.

It had a fine, forceful secretary in William Allen, who was appointed on a full time basis. The members paid what was for those days a very

Members of the London Match Girls Union who went on strike in 1888. Considered a fit subject for a successful London 'musical' in the late 1960's.

high weekly subscription of a shilling (5p), and the funds built up were used to supply sickness pay, unemployment pay and old age benefits. It must be remembered that the first state benefits along these lines were not supplied until the Twentieth Century, so these payments were doubly important.

The Amalgamated Society of Engineers was composed of better paid workers, and this is typical of the other unions that appeared during this period. This was particularly true of the re-organized miners' association, and the Amalgamated Society of Carpenters and Joiners, who had modelled their organization on the A.S.E. Their secretary was Robert Applegarth, another great figure in this period of trade union activity. He was a typical Victorian figure in that in *Who's Who* he listed his recreation as 'work, more work, and still more work'. Rather less typically he was a radical, working tirelessly on behalf of the working man. He had plenty of courage. Once, when facing a formidable steel master in Sheffield on behalf of an earlier trade society of which he was secretary, the following conversation took place:

'You're from the Trade Union.'

'Yes.'

'Well I shall cut you short.'

'Please don't. I am only five foot two and that is short enough.'

Men like Applegarth and Allen got into the habit of meeting regularly in London. Other trade union secretaries joined this close knit group of T.U. leaders, which has become known as the Junta, and began to draw up general trade union policy, thus

paving the way for the first Trades Union Congress, an annual meeting of representatives from every member union, which was held in 1868. Before this first meeting took place, however, the trade unions found themselves facing a major crisis. In Sheffield, in 1866, a worker who had refused to join a union had his house damaged by gunpowder, and other workers had their tools destroyed for similar reasons. At about the same time it was discovered that a union secretary had misused union funds and the union found that they could not prosecute because in the eyes of the law the unions were not regarded as Friendly Societies (Insurance Organizations). Applegarth and Allen were among the first to try to stamp out the Sheffield disgraces, but the middle and upper classes had been alarmed. A commission of inquiry was called for. The unions themselves, shattered by the discovery that their funds were not protected, tried to turn the Royal Commission to their advantage, and pressed for reforms of the laws covering trade union activities.

Owing to the steadiness of the Trade Unionists who gave evidence to the Royal Commission, particularly Applegarth, the Royal Commission report was by no means as unfavourable as it might have been. Gladstone's Liberal government passed a Trade Union Act in 1871. This act recognized Trade Unions as Friendly Societies and did not prohibit strikes, but it did bar peaceful picketing— that is the grouping of strikers round the entrance of a factory in order to persuade any non-strikers that they should join the strike. But the frustration of the Trade Unions at this prohibition was ended in 1875 when Disraeli's Conservative government passed the Conspiracy and Protection of Property Act allowing peaceful picketing—although the peaceful part has proved rather difficult to maintain at times.

Membership card of the International Working Men's Association 1869—signed by Karl Marx.

So, by the mid 1870's, the Trade Unions were firmly established with full legal protection, and were able to continue more fully their struggle to improve the lot of the working classes. However, most of their work continued to be on behalf of the better paid workers. A feature of the 1880's and 1890's was the growth of another form of unionism: that of the unskilled workers. Tea porters and general labourers at the docks in London banded together under the leadership of Ben Tillet. The match girls of Bryant & May formed a Union and took part in a famous strike in 1888 which resulted in higher wages for them. Then in 1889 came the strike of the London dockers for a minimum wage of sixpence ($2\frac{1}{2}$p) an hour. Subscriptions poured in from home and abroad, the Roman Catholic Cardinal Manning threw his weight behind the dockers and eventually they were successful.

Other unskilled unions appeared in the next few years and at the annual Trade Union Congresses some trade unionists began to demand that Unions should work towards the creation of a socialist society.

Education

The working man who was intent upon improving himself could expect little help from the state at this time. We have already seen how Trade Unions tried to provide some sort of security against the perils of sickness, unemployment and the onset of old age because of the lack of state provision such as we have today. Similarly in education the poorer sections of the community had to educate themselves.

Some elementary education *was* available. There were some fee paying 'schools' charging fees of up to ninepence (about 4p) a week but, even so, they often consisted only of a garret run by a child minder. More frequently found were the schools of the National Society, founded by Dr. Bell in 1811, a Church of England organization, or perhaps the schools of the British and Foreign Schools Society started by Joseph Lancaster in 1814 for nonconformists. Both Societies concentrated quite naturally on religious instruction, but in addition they did provide some training in reading, writing and arithmetic. The teaching method was primitive but cheap. One master taught a lesson to monitors who then passed it on to other groups. Thus it was said that one master could teach sixty or eighty pupils. One can imagine the bedlam, and also the lack of success. Children might stay at one of these schools for a period of three years, but little could be learned under such

a system. Mechanical lists of answers were parroted out to visiting inspectors who sometimes changed the questions round, but still received the answers in the original order.

The government gave some meagre help when in 1833 it granted £20 000 to the Societies. In 1839 it increased the grant to £30 000. In contrast, however, slave owners in the British empire received £20 000 000 compensation from the government when slavery was abolished in 1833.

By the middle of the century the government was paying about £150 000 to the two Societies to help them in their work, and some basic teacher training was also being carried out. Some of our present teacher training colleges stem from the institutions set up by the Churches to train teachers for their schools. Pupil teacher training was also in operation whereby more promising pupils continued their education whilst being trained as teachers at the same time.

In 1858 a government inquiry discovered that about one eighth of the population was attending some sort of school, although the real figure may have been much lower. In any case most of these children left school before the age of twelve, and the standard of education remained very low; so low, in fact, that the government decided to bring into education the methods of the factory system. Payment of government money was to be continued, but it was to be paid on results only. Attendance of pupils and an elementary test by visiting inspectors were to be considered in determining the amount of money received by an individual school. Thus mechanical learning continued as teachers, fearful of losing the grant, forced pupils to cram for the exam, and some

Poor boy reading his lessons in a late 19th. century London Board School.

lingering awe of the importance of the attendance register has remained in education up to our own day. There could be little hope of genuine willingness to learn while this system lasted, and it did not disappear for thirty years.

Education becomes Compulsory

A growing uneasiness over the state of education in England in the 1860's finally caused the government to step in and provide schools maintained out of rates and taxes. The Forster Education Act of 1870 set out to 'complete the present voluntary system, to fill up gaps...not to destroy the existing system'. In other words, where the voluntary societies had been unable to provide an adequate accommodation, then the state would provide the necessary school. Attendance was only compulsory if the schoolboard elected by local ratepayers decided upon such a step. By contrast with the Church Schools an undenominational course of religious education was to be given. Fees, admittedly small, were to be charged, for the Victorian view was that if something was free it would not be valued—an idea perhaps too easily dismissed in our own day. Two further Acts of Parliament in 1876 and 1880 finally made education compulsory, and in 1891 fees were abolished. Of course such a move was resented by some parents and children. The men from the schoolboard who came round to investigate absence were often looked upon with

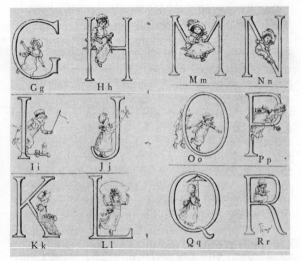

Pages from Kate Greenaway's school spelling book, 1885.

hatred by parents hoping to send their children out to work. But for some children from the foul slums of the industrial cities of Britain, the board school provided a haven of refuge from the appalling conditions at home, and in 1902 when the Balfour Education Act put the control of education in the hands of the County Councils it became possible for some working class children to obtain scholarships to grammar schools.

Parliamentary Help

The really important point about the previous section is to notice the way in which the State, in the shape of the government, began to take an increasing share in the work of providing education, refusing to leave it in the hands of voluntary organizations. It is just one example of the way that, by the 1860's, Parliament itself was beginning to recognize the need for change. It was even prepared to reform its own workings, for in 1866 Gladstone and the Whigs tried to bring in a Reform Bill designed to give the vote to an extra half million electors. This was narrowly defeated, but in the following year Disraeli and the Conservatives passed a much more far-reaching reform. This Act of 1867 was one of the most important measures of the century, for it went some way to meeting the old Chartist demand for universal suffrage by giving the vote to the skilled industrial worker. Under the terms of the Act all male householders in the towns and all lodgers who paid £10 a year in rent were allowed to vote at parliamentary elections. After 1867 the two main parties, the Conservatives and the Liberals (as the Whigs had become known), had to try to get the support of

Poor children being rounded up by the London School Board 'Kiddie-catcher' and a policeman at 2.40 in the morning, 1871.

these new voters. The two great party leaders, both knew this, and it is no coincidence that the Education Act of 1870 came only three years after this reform act. Forster's own words showed this. 'Now that we have given them [the skilled workers] political power, we must not wait any longer to give them education'.

When Disraeli's Conservative party took office in 1874 there was a flurry of reforms designed to continue the work of laying the foundations for a civilized social life. Disraeli believed that it was no good depending on unaided private efforts to improve social conditions. As far as he was concerned the basic freedoms of an Englishman should not include the freedom to live in squalor. An Artisans Dwelling Act emphasised the need for slum clearance and provided for the appointment of Medical Officers of Health. The great Public Health Act of 1875 'dealt with drains' but it was high time that an Act of Parliament *did* deal with drains. Such topics as refuse disposal, water supplies, public baths and compulsory notification of infectious diseases were covered by this great measure associated with the name of Richard Cross. It provided the basis for our laws on sanitation down to the 1930's. Joseph Chamberlain, the radical Lord Mayor of Birmingham, had

Slums in Newcastle on Tyne in the 1870's. These rickety houses look almost medieval and must have been riddled with damp and vermin.

Nineteenth century 'back-to-back' houses still standing in Rochdale at the end of the Second World War.

Rochdale road, Manchester in the late 19th. century.

already shown what could be done by someone energetic enough to make use of Cross's Artisans' Dwellings Act and the powers given to town councils by the 1835 Act which reformed municipal government. In three years from 1873 to 1876 Chamberlain claimed that Birmingham was 'parked, paved, assized, marketed, Gas-and-Watered and *improved*'. In one vast clearance scheme over 16 hectares of sub-standard property was swept away and replaced by the aptly named Corporation Street. It must also be remembered

that it was during this period of Disraeli's Ministry that trade Unions gained the right of peaceful picketing and that education finally became compulsory—working men, and skilled working men especially, were the beneficiaries.

State intervention in social conditions continued with further factory laws in 1877 and 1878. The responsibilities of the inspectors were increased and the weekly work maximum for woman was fixed at fifty-six and a half hours in textile factories and sixty in other types of factory. No child under ten was to be employed at all and, by the end of the century, this level had been raised to twelve. In addition, all employees benefited by the Employers Liability Act of 1897, by which employees received full protection against industrial accidents.

This same period saw the first important step in the battle for pure food. The right of some individual food makers and sellers to poison their customers was of course long established. The food and drug act of 1875 did make a start in prohibiting the inclusion of 'ingredients injurious to health'. The fight still goes on in our own day, though now usually over more complicated issues such as artificial sweeteners and preservatives.

With Gladstone returned to power in the early 1880's the issues rather shifted back to constitutional rights. In 1884 came the third electoral Reform Act extending to the countryside the voting regulations which had applied in the towns since 1867. The beneficiaries of this act were the

The smoke and grime of the great steel town of Sheffield in 1884.

Agricultural labourers, miners and other workmen who lived outside the larger towns. Four years later, by the 1888 County Councils Act, Lord Salisbury, the Conservative Prime Minister, brought county areas into line with the towns as regards local government by allowing elected councils to take over the administration of the counties. In 1894 Gladstone improved this system by subdividing the counties into urban, rural and parish districts which were also to be governed by elected councils chosen by the rate payers. One interesting feature of these reforms was the part women were allowed to play in the new arrangements. From 1882 onwards women could vote at town council elections and this was extended to county elections in 1888. In 1894 Gladstone went a stage further and allowed women not only the right to vote, but also to serve on the new district councils he had created. This was in sharp contrast to the refusal which always met women's demands for the right to vote in Parliamentary elections.

In general then, the picture of this period is one of continued State intervention on behalf of the

The heart of Birmingham after the Victorian improvers had done their work.

This photograph was taken of housing conditions in Manchester in the 1950's.

individual balancing the increased civil rights gained by the individual. The days of rampant *laissez-faire* were dead. State interference in the fields of factory reforms, trade union rights, and slum clearance was fully accepted. Indeed as the nineteenth century came to a close the question of old age pensions was under active debate and, although such a scheme was said to be too costly at the time, the demand for such a pension was to be granted only a few years later as one of the first steps towards what we call today the Welfare State (see glossary).

QUESTIONS

1. a) What do you understand by the term New Model Trade Unionism? What contribution to this movement were made by William Allen and Robert Applegarth?
   b) Explain the importance of the Acts of Parliament relating to Trade Unions passed in 1871 and in 1875.
2. Say why the following dates are important in the history of education – a) 1811, b) 1814, c) 1833, d) 1858, e) 1870, f) 1876, g) 1891.
3. Make a list of the important social reforms passed by Disraeli's government. Show how this scope has been increased during the present day.

SECTION 4

The New Century

This section takes the social and economic development of Great Britain up to the present day.

At the beginning of this century, most of the features typical of our present way of life had already appeared, although often in a primitive stage of development. The internal combustion engine had already been in existence for some years, but few could have forecast the changes it would bring, not only as a means of transport and the creator of important new industries, but also as the creator of such social problems as air pollution and inadequate road systems. The present century has also seen the extensive development in the use of electricity in the provision of electric trains, electrical power and a host of household usages.

Hopes of social progress were reflected by the further development of the creed of socialism, the appearance of the Labour Party as a new political force, and also by the desire of women to gain equal rights. In some respects however, it was a period which saw a widely fluctuating pattern of social progress. The provision of the Welfare State is described in the following chapters, but so is the Great Depression of the later 1920's and 1930's. Britain also had to contend with the shattering after-effects of two mighty world wars. There was also the gloomy picture given by the steady decline of the basic industries of this country, coal, iron and cotton, whose advance had been at the heart of the first industrial revolution, but which gradually were to lose their former importance as technological changes and foreign competition took away their usefulness and their competitiveness.

The period ends to some extent on a brighter note with the steadily increasing importance of newer industries, such as electronics, aeroplanes, plastics, motor cars and also the development of new power sources, in particular North Sea oil. However, Britain's inability to achieve a satisfactory balance between her imports and exports remains as one of the most urgent problems facing the country.

14   THE NEW CENTURY

In some ways the first World War of 1914–1918 seems to be the real ending of the nineteenth century. Yet most of the important features of the social and economic life of our own day had made their appearance in the decades immediately before 1914. The invention of the internal combustion engine and the consequent development of the aeroplane and the motor car, and the increased use of electricity for lighting and power were some of the outstanding features of the technical advances of the times. It was also a period that saw a renewed interest in socialism (see glossary), the appearance of the British Labour party as a new force in politics, vigorous Trade Union activity and the beginning of the Welfare State.

The Trade Unions and Socialism

The influential trades union leaders mentioned in the previous chapter were working towards well-defined ends within the existing system such as wage rises and shorter working days. But the widespread depression of the 1870's and 1880's had made men wonder whether a capitalist society could survive after all. Two German socialists, Karl Marx and Frederick Engels, were living in England at this time. Engels, who came from a wealthy German family engaged in the textile industry, had spent some time in Manchester and had seen for himself the depressing conditions of life for the factory hands whose work supplied the profit for the factory owner. He had later helped Karl Marx, with advice, and more important, with money, while Marx produced his famous book *Das Kapital*. Marx wrote the book in London and continued to live in England after it was published (he is buried in Highgate cemetery in London). The main theme of this book was that the misery

The playwright George Bernard Shaw in the 1880's when he was a leading Fabian.

James Keir Hardie, a founder of the modern Labour Party.

of working class life sprang from the fact that industry was organized on a capitalist (see glossary) basis which made private profit the main motive for all business enterprise. This would inevitably mean that the private owners of industry would try to get the most out of their workers and give the least in return. The solution for Marx, was to overthrow such a system so that the workers, through control of the State, would take over the ownership of all private industry and land for the benefit of the whole community.

Marx was putting forward a theory of warfare by one class, the workers, against another class, the owners of industry. In Britain however, the renewed interest in Socialism which *Das Kapital* helped to foster took a non-violent form, laying emphasis on gradual change rather than sudden revolution—in fact attempting to achieve socialism by use of democratic parliamentary methods.

The Fabian Society, formed in 1884, was such a group. Their name was taken from the Roman General Fabius, renowned for his patience in waiting for the right moment to strike, their motto was the 'inevitability of gradualness', their methods consisted of getting themselves known by writing essays and pamphlets. Such a writer was George Bernard Shaw. A typical speech of Shaw's at a Fabian conference, in which he attacked shareholders and landlords, went as follows:

'He was about to refer to a modern class, the burglars, but if there was a burglar present he begged him to believe that he cast no reflection upon his profession . . . or finally of the great number

of people to whom he gave employment, including criminal attorneys, policemen, turnkeys, builders of gaols, and it might be the hangman. He did not wish to hurt the feelings of shareholders . . . or of landlords. . . . He would merely point out that all three inflicted on the community an injury of precisely the same nature'. Two or three years before the Fabians had commenced publishing their socialist lectures a wealthy stockbroker, H. M. Hyndman, had founded the Social Democratic Federation. It is curious perhaps that a wealthy stockbroker should have become attracted to the idea of a socialist controlled state with public ownership of industry, but Hyndman seemed to have been converted by reading Marx's *Das Kapital*.

You will have noticed that both Hyndman and the Fabians did not spring from what the Victorians called 'the labouring classes'. However, the trade unions at this time were beginning once again to be influenced by socialist ideas. This was an important fact for the unions had begun to put forward working class candidates at parliamentary elections. Indeed by 1886 there were eleven of these union-sponsored M.P.'s, although they sat in the House of Commons as members of the Liberal Party. In 1892 James Keir Hardie, a Scottish miners' leader, joined them. Keir Hardie was the son of a carpenter who went to work at the age of seven. As a lad he lost a job because he was a few minutes late, the lateness being caused by death in his family. The lecture he received for his lateness before his dismissal was something he never forgot. After a spell of work as a miner he successfully organized a

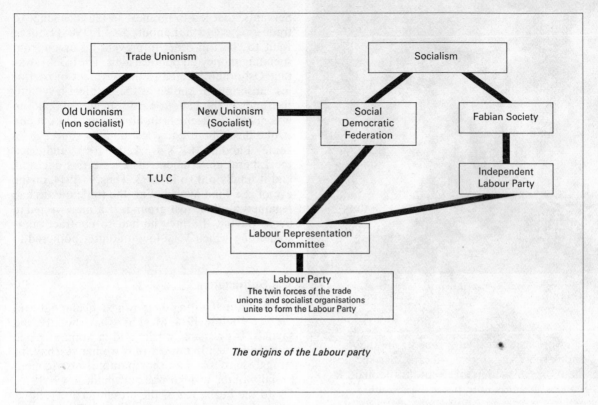

The origins of the Labour party

Miners' Union. After his election to the House of Commons Keir Hardie became convinced that it was no use being attached to the coat tails of the Liberal Party. Hardie knew that the Bradford Labour Union had actually run Ben Tillet as a candidate against the Liberal member for East Bradford and he was anxious that this and other labour movements should get together.

In 1893 a conference at Bradford under Keir Hardie's leadership led to the formation of the Independent Labour Party, the 'I.L.P.' In 1895 it put up 28 candidates. All were defeated and the cause of working men M.P.'s seemed to be worse off than ever. Better backing and more money was needed and Keir Hardie's hopes received a boost when an I.L.P. man was elected to the post of General Secretary of the Amalgamated Society of Engineers. A grand conference in London in 1900 between the I.L.P., Fabians and Trade Unionists produced the 'Labour Representation Committee'. Its secretary was J. Ramsay MacDonald. The Committee succeeded in getting two members (one was Keir Hardie) elected in 1900, and in 1906 28 members of the group that had become known simply as the Labour Party were elected. Three years later a further 24 M.P.'s who had been elected with the backing of various unions joined forces with the Labour group, and so a powerful

new force emerged in British politics; but it was a force that was in the main interested in the non-violent achievement of socialism.

Difficult Years for the Unions

One of the reasons why the unions had shown a keenness to support the formation of a Labour Party in the House of Commons was a challenge that had arisen to the very basis of the Trade Unions in 1901. The Taff Vale Railway Company in South Wales sued the Amalgamated Society of Railway Servants for damages arising from a strike organized by the Union. The Union was ordered to pay £23 000 by the courts, and the significance of this judgement caused general dismay among trade unionists. Apparently trade union funds were not protected in any way by law after all. If a union could be sued successfully for the cost of a strike then the whole of a Union's funds would soon be drained away.

The infant Labour Party could do little by itself, but it could exercise influence on the great Liberal government that came to power in 1906. This government listened to the Labour Party's views on the Taff Vale case and brought in a trade union bill substantially giving the unions all the protection that they could have wished for their funds.

Greater opportunities for women. Men and women working together on chemical research at Leeds University in the early 1900's.

A strike could now take place without the danger of a trade union being held financially responsible for losses sustained by the employer. As Pauline Gregg says 'The Act of 1906 was a triumph for the trade unions and the Labour Party. To the trade unions it meant an assured freedom in their work; to the Labour party it brought an enhanced prestige'. It also gave the trade unions a privileged place in society and in law when they wished to strike.

The Osborne Judgement

Trade Union funds might be protected. Those of the Labour party were now to be challenged. The attack was not from the employers, although obviously capitalist employers would not sit idly while a party grew in power which was committed to socialist policies. Not all Trade Unionists by any means were socialist in opinion. Many working men had always voted Conservative, a fact that caused both Marx and Engels to sometimes despair of the English. There were many trade unionists who preferred to support the Liberals, and it was the action of W. C. Osborne, a liberal trade unionist branch secretary of the Amalgamated Railway Servants, that led to the next serious challenge to trade unions and the Labour party. In 1908 Osborne went to court in order to prevent his union from spending money on political aims. The trouble was that Osborne objected to the payment of part of his subscription, known as the political levy, into the funds of the Labour party. On appeal Osborne was given a judgement in his favour. Thus at one stroke the Labour party lost a major source of income. Labour M.P.'s worked hard to influence the Liberal government to reverse this decision, and it finally did so in 1913. Thus, in 1914, on the eve of the First World War, the trade unions had regained all their lost ground. If a man wished to avoid paying the levy he had to contract out— something which very few unionists bothered to do.

The Suffragettes

Women were fighting their own particular battle in the years before 1914. Most of us have heard of the sayings 'It's a mans' world' and 'a woman's place is in the home'. In our own day women still have to struggle hard to achieve comparable status to men. Equal pay for women was only made law in 1975. Up to the beginning of the present century, however, the situation was far worse. The pioneers of the struggle for equality and the emancipation of women faced great difficulties. One of the first lady doctors, Elizabeth Garrett Anderson, had to train privately because no medical school would accept her as a student. Indeed until women's colleges were specifically set up, a University education was virtually impossible. (It was only in 1968 that Oxford accepted a woman as president of the Oxford Union). Some men did give help; Bernard Shaw, for instance, hammered away at the topic in many of the plays he wrote towards the end of the nineteenth century.

The introduction of the typewriter and the telephone created thousands of office jobs, particularly in London, and this fact helped to make it easier for single girls to go out to work after finishing their education. 'The new women', as they were known, began to take part in cycling and tennis, but very few women could be satisfied with the rate of progress towards equality, especially as one of the most basic rights, that of the vote, was denied to them.

In 1903 Mrs. Emmeline Pankhurst and her daughter Cristobel founded the Women's Political and Social Union. Their aim was to gain the right to vote, the suffrage, hence the term suffragettes. To begin with she and her followers were content

Suffragettes with sandwich boards in London during the General Election campaign of January 1910. The posters are anti-Liberal to the government of the day. But the Conservatives were not any the less opposed to women's suffrage.

to interrupt political meetings and stage protest marches, but more violent methods were adopted when no recognition of their aim had been gained. Women chained themselves to the railings outside No. 10 Downing Street. Priceless paintings in the National Gallery were slashed (the Rokeby Venus being perhaps the most famous example). Letter boxes were blown up, and women who were sent to prison sometimes went on hunger strike and were forcibly fed by the prison authorities—a repellant technique. One suffragette did die for her beliefs. Emily Davison threw herself under the King's horse in the 1913 Derby. All this was, however, in vain, and did more harm than good. More thoughtful suffragists began to turn back to the less spectacular but painstaking societies that preferred to use constitutional means. In the same year that Emily Davison killed herself, the National Union of Suffrage Societies spent over £45 000 on a well-organized campaign designed to influence public and parliamentary opinion.

Even so, when women finally gained the vote in 1918 it was more as a result of their contribution to the war effort from 1914 onwards, than as a direct result of pressure, militant or constitutional, before the First World War.

The Social Scene

The old thought that 'the rich get rich and the poor get poorer' was never more true than in the years immediately leading up to the First World War. For a privileged few, Edwardian England, as this period is sometimes termed, seemed to be a never ending round of dinner parties, 'coming out' balls and weekend country house parties. Even the weather (according to the reminiscences of those who lived through this period) seemed to produce a period of brilliant summers. John Galsworthy's novel, *The Forsyte Saga*, showed that sort of life open not only to the aristocracy but also to the richer middle class (the plutocracy).

Other writers emphasized other aspects. The life of the servants of these people could often represent the other extreme. One servant's room, for instance, was described as follows 'The room had a slanting roof and was whitewashed . . . there was a rusty grate, an old iron bedstead and a hard bed covered with a faded coverlet. Some pieces of furniture too much worn to be used downstairs had been sent up'.

The contrast presented by master and servant mirrored the whole contrast of life in Edwardian England. The average weight of working class boys was 11 lbs (5 kilogrammes) less than that of boys from wealthy families. Their height on average was 5 ins (127 millimetres) less. The infant mortality rate at the beginning of the century showed 18% of children born in the west end of London dying before the age of 5. That is bad enough by today's

91

A painting to mark the introduction of Old Age Pensions in 1909.

standards, but in the East End 55% died before the age of five.

It is against this background that the importance of the first steps in providing what we would today term the Welfare State need to be measured. These steps were taken during the years immediately before the outbreak of the First World War, starting in 1906 when the Liberal Party was swept into power with a huge majority after eleven years out of office.

The Liberals had been helped by the effort of some Conservatives to bring back protective duties on trade, which had once again rallied the supporters of free trade. But they had also presented an election programme promising an attack on poverty and social reform. Lloyd-George the Liberal Chancellor of the Exchequer announced his purpose to be that of 'raising money to wage implacable warfare against poverty and squalidness'. *The Times* claimed that his proposals were 'half thought out arguments'. But to many old people the first great step did not seem to be so. A non-contributory old age pension (25p per week for a single person, 37½p for a married couple) was introduced in 1908. An eight hour day for miners was brought in during the same year. In 1909 an attempt was made to help fight the problem of

unemployment by establishing Labour Exchanges, so that unemployed persons could find out what work was available in their own district.

In 1911 the Liberal government tackled the problem of social insurance. The principles they followed had been in operation in Germany for a number of years; the Liberals' achievement was in successfully applying them in Britain. The National Insurance Act of 1911 introduced a scheme for contributory insurance. The Bill's aim was that the employer and the State should enter into a partnership with the working man in order to mitigate . . . the severity of the burden which falls upon him'. The scheme provided free medical attention for manual workers earning less than £160 a year. The partnership aspect arose from the fact that anyone who qualified for the benefits of the scheme paid 4d. a week into the fund and the employers paid 3d. (2.4d = 1p). The State made it up to 9d. by contributing a further 2d., and the money was used to pay doctors who accepted a certain number of free patients on their list or panel. Note, however, that the medical aid did not extend to the family of the panel patient, nor to any other section of the community. Nevertheless the Act marked a beginning of our present system which, heavily attacked though it is, is infinitely preferable to the Poor Law method of providing for sickness, unemployment and so on. Lloyd George, the minister responsible for framing the Act, seems to have half hoped that the aid could one day be free. This, of course, has not been possible, but Lloyd George was right when he recognized that his scheme would ultimately replace the Poor Law. A note of his, written in 1911, said that 'At no distant date I hope the State will acknowledge a full responsibility in the matter of making provision for sickness, breakdown and unemployment. It really does so now through Poor Law: but conditions . . . have been so harsh and degrading that working class pride revolts' . . .

A feature of the scheme was the introduction of the now familiar national insurance card with its weekly stamp recording the subscription paid. There was a well reported 'revolt of the duchesses' who held meetings in London to protest at having to 'lick' stamps for these new cards on behalf of their servants, who, incidentally, supported their masters in this protest. Some doctors refused to operate the scheme but the move collapsed because doctors operating the panel discovered they now received a steady income from the state.

The welfare of children also figured in the Liberal programme. In 1906 free school meals were instituted for very poor children. Medical inspection of schoolchildren began in the following year. Free milk was also provided until 1968.

The Technological Revolution

Steps such as those outlined above marked the beginning of a social revolution which was matched by a sweeping technological revolution, which similarly had its origins in the thirty years preceeding the outbreak of the First World War.

The telephone, wireless telegraphy, and electric lighting were all developed in the closing years of the nineteenth century and were gradually coming into use by 1914. Improvements made to the dynamo and the electric motor in the same period were followed by an increased use of electrical power in factories and by the introduction of electric tramways and electric railways, two of which, the London Tube and Liverpool Overhead Railway, were in operation almost ten years before Queen Victoria died.

At the same time inventors were working to perfect the movie camera, and the first cinemas appeared in the early 1900's showing short silent films like 'The Great Train Robbery', the first screen Western, made in America in 1903. By 1914 cinema audiences already had their favourite stars and one of these, Charlie Chaplin, has remained a favourite ever since. Even the atomic age was foreshadowed before 1914 in the work of people like Professor Röntgen, the German scientist who discovered X-rays in 1895, and Madame Curie, whose experiments with radioactive substances led to the discovery of radium in 1898. These developments were of immediate value to medical science, but they also had a wider importance in that they formed a part of some of the earliest research into nuclear physics which was being carried out at that time by the British scientists J. J. Thomson and Ernest Rutherford.

Perhaps the most important technical development of all during this period, was the invention of the internal combustion engine by the German engineer A. N. Otto. This discovery has probably had the greatest single impact on our everyday lives in the twentieth century, and when Gottlieb Daimler, Otto's former assistant, built what is generally regarded as the world's first motor-car in 1886 he began a transport revolution comparable with that caused by the introduction of the steam locomotive. This was not realized at the time, of course, because early motor-cars were expensive and unreliable, but they developed rapidly, particularly in France and the United States, where Henry Ford built his first car in 1893; and by the

An Edwardian traffic jam outside the Mansion House in London about 1910. Note the mixture of horse-drawn and motor vehicles.

end of the century motoring was well established in all the leading industrial nations. In Britain the sport of motoring became very popular in the Edwardian period, and pioneer engineers like Herbert Austin, William Morris, Henry Royce, and others laid the foundations of the modern motor-car industry at that time. By 1914 cars, lorries,

The first Rolls-Royce Silver Ghost built in 1907. This car is still in good running order and has done 800 000 kilometres to date.

C. Compton Paterson, one of the competitors in the 1911 £10 000 Round Britain Air Race sponsored by the Daily Mail.

motor-buses, and delivery vans were a common sight on our city streets and the internal combustion engine was soon to prove its worth in a variety of ways in the First World War.

Meanwhile the petrol engine had provided aviation pioneers with a compact, lightweight power unit and enabled them to realize the age-old dream of flight, and in December 1903 two American brothers, Orville and Wilbur Wright, made the first powered flight at Kitty Hawk in North Carolina. This memorable event went almost completely unrecorded at the time, but the Wright brothers were soon attracting world wide attention, particularly after a flight of 40 km in 1908. Soon others began to make similar flights in flimsy home-made aircraft, and in 1909 Blériot, a French pilot, made his famous crossing of the English Channel to collect the £1000 prize offered by the *Daily Mail* to the first man to achieve this feat. This sort of competition greatly stimulated public interest in aviation, and like motoring it developed rapidly. When Orville Wright died in 1912 flying was ceasing to be a sport for wealthy young men and was becoming established as an industry in its own right.

The First World War

The First World War, which broke out in August 1914, is sometimes regarded as the real end of the nineteenth century, the point which dates the beginning of the sweeping changes we associate with the twentieth century way of life. In fact the previous sections have shown that the foundations of our present type of society are to be found in the years preceeding the outbreak of war and that in addition many important technological changes were well under way by 1914.

What the coming of war did do, however, was to accelerate the rate of change in these fields. Perhaps most of all it subjected the people of Britain to a degree of control over their lives and property that they had never before experienced. This control only lasted for the length of the war but it reinforced the arguments of socialists in their desire to see, for instance, the state control major industries. Indeed Winston Churchill used the expression 'war socialism' to describe this period of government control.

In the early months of the war there was little evidence of what was to come. The government had passed the Defence of the Realm Act (D.O.R.A.) which gave the widest powers over civilians and the armed forces, but for the mass of the population the war was still something 'over there' in France. At least it was until German warships shelled Scarborough, and in December 1914 a Zeppelin airship carried out the first bombing raid on Britain. In April 1915 London was bombed and there were further raids by airships and aeroplanes which caused over a thousand deaths by the end of the war. Trivial figures perhaps by the standards of the Second World War, but nevertheless a fact showing the arrival of total war with civilians in the front line and liable to be in just as much danger as the troops at the 'Front'.

Much of this lay in the future. For the privileged life still went on as it had done before the war. As A. J. P. Taylor said 'Statesmen still appeared in top hats. Business men rarely lapsed into bowlers. Some standards were slightly relaxed. Short black jackets took the place of tail coats for evening dress. Some men wore unstarched collars at the weekend. Maidservants instead of footmen handed round the sandwiches at afternoon tea and were to be seen even in West End clubs.'

Yet the government was facing pressing problems. There was a manpower crisis in the forces owing to the failure of the early rush of volunteers to keep pace with the slaughter of the troops in France. There was a shortage of shipping caused by the devastatingly successful German submarine attacks. This indeed was a critical shortage, for it affected our ability to continue the war whether or not our armies remained undefeated. There was no proper system of allocation of Britain's available manpower to the tasks involved in modern war, for instance in the manufacturing of munitions and the maintainance of communications. The country felt that there was no real drive in tackling these matters and at the end of 1916, Lloyd-George became Prime Minister.

Conscription had been introduced some months earlier and a Ministry of Munitions had been set up, but the new government took drastic action. New government departments were created. Three new Ministries were set up, those of Labour, Shipping and National Service. There was also a Department of Food. Their powers were wide. For instance merchant ships, their movements and their cargoes were now strictly controlled. The mines were taken over for the duration of the war. This nationalization of the mines was to be a cause of trouble in the future when the miners wanted them to remain in public ownership after the end of the war. Food rationing was finally introduced in 1918. Bread was not included although its price was subsidized to the amount of £60 000 000 a year. In fact there was a general control of prices in the interests of the lower paid. Rents were also held at their pre-war level.

Nevertheless 1917 and 1918 were doleful years for many with 1917 being perhaps the worst year of the war. There was more real shortage in food because of the German submarines in that year than there was in 1918 when food rationing was officially introduced, and when the U-Boats had been beaten. Queues for food and for fuel became a feature of life and trains were slow and crowded. There was wide resentment against the 'profiteers', the men who were making huge profits out of armaments and those who were able to take advantage of wartime shortages.

By 1918 life in Britain was controlled by the state in a manner never before experienced by civilians. Committees of the Cabinet allocated the available manpower of the whole country according to the needs of the army, navy, airforce, munitions production, timber felling, the growing of food and so on. This was state planning on a scale never before attempted by this country.

Thus when the war ended, Britain had experienced conscription of men, had seen women take over a vast range of jobs previously handled by men only, and had operated the principle of nationalization in the mines. Although the ending of the war saw a great attempt by the privileged classes to revert to the sort of life and the type of social system that they had known before 1914, Britain could never be quite the same again.

QUESTIONS

1. a) Describe the steps leading up to the formation of the Labour Party.
   b) Find out from reference books as much as you can about George Bernard Shaw and Keir Hardie.
2. What was the importance of
   a) the Taff Vale Case 1901
   and
   b) the Osborne Case, in the development of Trade Unions?
3. Describe some of the important stages in the struggle for the emancipation of women.
4. What evidence is there in the chapter of a great gulf between rich and poor? What steps did the Liberal Government take between the years 1906–1914 to help the poorer sections of the community?
5. In what ways did the British Government direct and control the lives of the people of Britain during the First World War?

15 BRITAIN BETWEEN THE WARS (I), 1919–1929

The First World War ended on November 11th 1918 and crowds danced in the streets of London to celebrate the victory. It had been a long hard struggle in which more than three quarters of a million men from the British Isles had given their lives, but now it was all over most people looked forward to the future with confidence. They believed that they had been fighting to build a better world and, now that the killing had stopped, they wished to get down to the task of creating something worthwhile out of the ruins. These feelings seemed to be underlined by the politicians. In the general election which immediately followed the armistice Lloyd George, the Prime Minister, promised that if he was returned to power he would make Britain a 'fit country for heroes to live in' and on the basis of this promise and his enormous prestige as a wartime leader Lloyd George and his supporters were re-elected.

The Post War Boom

At first it seemed that the politicians' promises would be fulfilled. Trade began to pick up in the spring of 1919 and Britain was soon enjoying a full scale industrial boom. The shipyards were busy

Armistice celebrations in London when the First World War ended in November 1918.

making good wartime losses, exports of coal and machinery to war-shattered European countries like France and Belgium rose month by month, and at home people were anxious to buy the household goods and luxury items which had been in short supply during the war. As a result both wages and profits rose and the men coming back from the war had no difficulty in obtaining jobs. Then, in 1921, the bubble burst. All the ships that were needed had been built, the industries of the European countries had got back into production and the demands of the home market were satisfied. Almost overnight the boom turned into a slump and by the summer of 1921 more than two million men were unemployed. The legacy of enormous economic difficulties facing Britain as a result of the war was at last clear.

Economic Difficulties

The chief problem was exports. During the war, while Britain concentrated on war production, many of our best overseas customers had either turned elsewhere to buy goods previously obtained from us, or they had begun to manufacture them for themselves. As a result much of our trade in the Far East had been taken over by Japan, our market in South America was lost to the United States, while in India a flourishing home textile industry reduced the amount of cotton cloth the Indians needed to buy from Lancashire. In addition many of the new small European states created at the end of the war, such as Czechoslovakia, began to build up their own industries for reasons of national pride. To protect these new industries they erected high tariff barriers against foreign goods, and so traditional suppliers like Britain were kept out. In these new conditions Britain fount it very much harder to sell, and the volume of our exports in 1919 was 45% below what it had been in 1913.

The other big problem was debt. The British government had raised large loans to finance the war (to the United States alone we owed £850 000 000) and simply to pay the interest meant

'A country fit for heroes.' Unemployed workers queue for their dole outside a Labour Exchange in the 1920's.

finding £326 000 000 each year. The normal method of repaying large international debts of this kind is through the export of goods, and this imposed a very heavy burden on British industry throughout the 1920's. The war had thus completely destroyed the old economic supremacy which Britain had enjoyed in the nineteenth century and the 'country fit for heroes' was going to be very hard to achieve.

Industry and Unemployment

The industries most affected by the changed economic circumstances after 1918 were the basic exporting industries of coal, textiles, iron and steel, shipbuilding and heavy engineering. They suffered from the general decline of world trade in the impoverished years after the war, from the loss of many traditional markets and from one other factor—by 1918 these industries were in many ways out of date. The war had stimulated the twentieth century technological revolution and, in the years after the war, oil and electricity began to replace coal, motor cars and lorries replaced railways, and artificial fibres and plastics began to replace cotton and other traditional materials. For these reasons the world did not want Britain's staple products in anything like the old quantities, especially as they were often expensive because of out of date methods and old fashioned machinery. The inevitable result was heavy unemployment in the old industrial regions on the coalfields. In August 1922 60% of the labour force at Hartlepool was out of

work, and in nearby Stockton-on-Tees 49% were without jobs. The same percentage was idle in the shipbuilding town of Barrow-in-Furness and unemployment figures were high all over industrial Scotland, in South Wales and in Lancashire. Over the country as a whole the numbers out of work never fell below a million at any time between 1921 and 1939.

The Dole

The very heavy unemployment put a great strain on the National Insurance scheme, introduced by Lloyd George in 1911 to protect workers in trades like building where seasonal unemployment was common. In 1920 it had been extended to cover workers in most other industries as well. In all some eleven million men were included. After the slump set in this system became unworkable because many men found themselves out of work for months at a time, and so it became necessary to make extra payments beyond the original fifteen weeks that the scheme had provided for. This extra benefit which was introduced in 1921 became known as the 'dole' and to obtain it a man had to 'sign on' at the local labour exchange three times a week to prove he was genuinely seeking work. He was then entitled to draw his dole on a Friday. Some historians have suggested that the dole saved England from revolution in the difficult years of the early twenties. This may or may not be true, but what is certain is that the dole was the

97

THE INCITEMENT: A GREAT CROWD BEING ADDRESSED BY DAVID KIRKWOOD, ONE OF THE STRIKE LEADERS, WHO HAS BEEN ARRESTED

WINDOWS WERE SMASHED for showing lights.

SEVERAL TRAMWAY CARS were also damaged.

SIGNALLERS ON A ROOF

ST. GEORGE'S SQUARE, THE SCENE OF THE BATON CHARGE

GUARDING A RAILWAY BRIDGE

THE RESULTS: AN INJURED POLICEMAN

A BATON CHARGE INCIDENT

KIRKWOOD BEING BROUGHT ROUND AFTER THE CHARGE

The 'battle' of St. George's Square – labour troubles in Glasgow. A page from The Graphic, February 8th. 1919.

only thing which stood between a great many working class families and the workhouse.

The Labour Movement

Not surprisingly, in view of the prevailing economic conditions, there was considerable labour unrest in the period after the First World War. In the months immediately following the armistice this was reflected by the revolutionary fever which swept over the whole of Europe as a result of the success of the Communist (see glossary) revolution in Russia; but after 1921 and the onset of the slump, the unrest was prompted by more immediate grievances such as the imposition of wage cuts and longer working hours. It expressed itself in two main ways. There were a great many strikes and industrial disputes, and there was also a dramatic increase in the number of votes cast at elections in support of the Labour Party.

The Labour Party, as we saw in Chapter 14, was formed specifically to represent the interests of the workers, and in the 1906 election 29 Labour members had been returned to the House of Commons. In the 1918 election this number had increased to 59 and in the election in 1922 it rose again to 142. In the next general election, in 1924, 191 Labour members were returned, giving the Labour Party a chance of power. Although they did not have an overall majority Ramsay MacDonald formed the first Labour Government in that year. It depended for its existence on the good will of the Liberals and it only lasted ten months, but this was long enough to prove that Labour ministers could govern, and from then on Labour replaced the Liberals as the alternative to Conservative rule. Ramsay MacDonald thus came back into office in 1929 at the head of a second Labour Government.

In the meantime the more direct battle for better conditions which was being waged by the trades unions had built up to the climax of the General Strike of 1926, a head-on clash between the unions and the government which we shall examine in the next section.

The General Strike

The General Strike arose out of trouble in the coal mining industry which fared very badly in the years after the war. During the war the miners had won better hours, pay and conditions when the mines were being worked flat out under government control, and when the war ended they had hoped that nationalization would become permanent. In 1921, however, the mines were handed back to their private owners who began to impose wage cuts to balance falling profits as trade declined. The miners resisted these efforts as vigorously as they could and labour relations in the industry broke down. Matters came to a head in 1925 when the miners, faced with a new round of pay cuts and an extension to their working day, threatened a national strike. The slogan of A. J. Cook, the miners' union leader, 'Not a penny off the pay, not a minute on the day' became the men's battle cry, and since neither they nor the owners would budge an inch there was complete deadlock. The government intervened and agreed to pay a subsidy to keep miner's wages the same while more negotiations were carried on, but these failed and so on May 1st 1926, the coal mining industry came to a halt. The men were told they must accept the owners' new agreements and when they refused they were locked out.

With wage cuts threatened in many other industries at the time, the Trades Union Congress decided

A food convoy being taken under armed guard from the East India Docks to the big food distribution centre in Hyde Park. The crowd seems to be watching in respectful silence.

that the time had come to fight and so they called a sympathetic strike of all key workers in support of the miners' claims. Transport workers, dockers, printers, workers in iron and steel and those in the gas and electricity supply industries all answered the T.U.C.'s call and the General Strike began at midnight on May 3rd 1926.

There had been talk of a full scale stoppage of this sort ever since 1921, and when it came Stanley Baldwin's Conservative government was well prepared. Civil Commissioners were ready in each area of the country to carry out the government's plans and everything went ahead very smoothly. Essential supplies were moved in convoys, where necessary under armed guard, and middle class volunteers were enrolled to act as special constables, train and 'bus drivers and to work in the docks and the power stations. The government began to publish its own newspaper, the 'British Gazette' edited by Winston Churchill, and this was cleverly used to present the government's case against the strikers.

The T.U.C. leaders were not nearly so well organized. Most of the work at Eccleston Square, the T.U.C. headquarters, fell to a few active men like Ernest Bevin who quickly became worn out with the strain and worry, while the more moderate union leaders grew more and more alarmed at what they had done. To rally the strikers and present the union side of the case the T.U.C. published its own newspaper called the British Worker and up and down the country local union branches worked hard to ensure that the stoppage was complete. Before long, however, a serious dispute arose as to

who should negotiate on the miners' behalf, and when the miners' leaders insisted on retaining this right for themselves the T.U.C. decided to call the Strike off. It had lasted nine days.

At the local level, where the stoppage had been almost 100% solid and where there had been some brilliantly improvised organization, the T.U.C. decision came as a dreadful blow. The men felt their leaders had betrayed them and thousands left the trades union movement in disgust in the weeks that followed. As for the miners, they fought on alone until the autumn when, with their funds exhausted and their wives and children starving, they were driven back to work on the owners'

Barbed wire being draped over the bonnet of a bus to stop strikers from attacking the driver during the General Strike in 1926. Note how troops were used to guard bus depots.

terms. The great battle between organized labour and the government had ended in defeat for the workers and in the following year the government pressed home its advantage by making general strikes illegal and by altering the system by which the Labour Party collected most of its funds. (See Chapter 14). Many people regarded these as unnecessary acts of spite, and the workers did not forget. At the next general election Baldwin was defeated and a Labour Government was returned to power, without, however, an overall majority.

Progress

So far the picture we have painted of the 1920's has been rather a gloomy one, but the period did have its brighter side. There was for example very considerable progress in many new industries. It did not balance the decline in the older industries, hence the high unemployment, but significant advances were made. The rayon industry, the manufacture of electrical goods, chemicals, stainless steel, scientific instruments and plastics, all forged ahead in the twenties, and the motor industry made particularly good progress. William Morris's works at Cowley, near Oxford, and Herbert Austin's plant at Longbridge outside Birmingham, became important new industrial centres. Car production as a whole went up from 32 000 vehicles in 1920 to 182 000 in 1929, and this in turn stimulated the home rubber industry manufacturing tyres and led to the growth of components firms supplying such items as batteries and brake linings. Much of this new industry relied on electrical power, and so many of the new factories were built in the midlands and the south, near to the great home market of London rather than on the coalfields in the north; a significant change in the location of British industry.

The twenties also brought considerable social advance. Scientific developments like electricity and the motor car made life easier and more pleasant and in many of the new industries wages were good. As a result more people had more money to spend on household appliances like vacuum cleaners, and on new entertainments like the cinema, radio and greyhound racing which blossomed as a spectator sport after its introduction to Britain in 1926. Many people also had more money to spend on housing and there was a boom in the building trade as a result. Thousands of families in the twenties moved out of dark Victorian terraces into bright new homes on the outskirts, an increasing number of which were lit and heated

An Austin 7. The first model of the famous 'peoples car' which appeared in the 1920's.

by electricity after the establishment of the National Grid in 1926. Many of these new homes were provided by the local authorities who received direct financial help from the government under the terms of the Addison Housing Act 1919 and the Wheatley Housing Act 1924.

Women fared particularly well in the twenties enjoying a new freedom and emancipation which was reflected in the boyish, practical clothes of the period. They had taken over countless jobs during the war to release men for the fighting, and at the end of the war much of the old prejudice against women having an equal place with men in society had gone. In 1918 women over 30 were given the vote and in 1919 the first woman (Nancy Astor) entered Parliament. In 1928 the voting age was reduced to 21, giving women equal political rights with men, and in the following year Margaret Bondfield became the first woman cabinet minister when she was appointed Minister of Labour by Ramsay MacDonald.

One final improvement in the 20's was the complete reorganization of the Poor Law as part of the 1929 Local Government Act. The hated workhouses and the Boards of Guardians which had existed for almost a century were swept away, and paupers were classified properly and dealt with in different institutions run by the local authorities. The sick went to hospitals, the aged to old peoples homes, children to orphanages run by the local education committees and so forth. The old 'bastilles' were either pulled down or modernized and turned into hospitals.

Conclusion

Thus for a great many people the twenties brought a better life, and standards of living generally were higher than ever before. Unfortunately a lot of working class families were left behind. Unemployment and low wages in many of the old industries brought poverty and squalor which was a long way from the dream of a 'fit country for heroes'. One middle class volunteer who enrolled as a special constable in 1926 during the General Strike was shocked by what he saw in the slums of London. 'I had never realized the appalling poverty which existed then in the Wandsworth, Nine Elms and Vauxhall districts—and probably elsewhere in London was just as bad. The squalor of those living conditions could not have been endured by anyone earning sufficient wages to get out of it'. Yet despite this, the twenties did end in a mood of cautious optimism, among businessmen at least. Trade picked up gradually from the beginning of 1925, and with exports rising and industrial production increasing it began to seem that complete economic recovery was possible. In 1929 when the unemployment figures for each month were lower than in the corresponding months of 1928, some people began to say that things were getting 'back to normal'. On this hopeful note the 1920's came to an end.

Fashion models demonstrating the latest styles in the 1920's.

QUESTIONS

1. Why was the First World War followed by a short industrial boom and why did it come to an end in 1921?
2. Why was it more difficult for Britain to sell her goods overseas in the period after 1918?
3. What was the 'dole' and why did it become necessary to introduce it in 1921?
4. Write an account of the General Strike of 1926 and say whether you would have been on the side of of the workers or the government had you been alive at that time. Give your reasons.
5. In what ways did life improve during the 1920's?
6. Why did female emancipation go ahead after 1918 when the Suffragettes had made such little progress before the First World War?

16 BRITAIN BETWEEN THE WARS (II), 1929–1939

The high hopes of complete economic recovery with which the 1920's ended were soon dashed by events. In October 1929 share prices suddenly collapsed on the New York Stock Exchange signalling the start of the worst economic crisis in modern history. The 'great depression' (see glossary) brought financial crashes in Germany and Austria, a catastrophic fall in the prices of almost all commodities, which ruined many producers, and a very sharp decline in world trade. A League of Nations Commission which investigated the matter estimated that by 1933 the depression had thrown thirty million men out of work in the leading industrial nations alone.

The Slump in Britain

As a trading nation Britain was automatically affected by the world wide economic crisis. The total value of our exports which stood at £839 millions in 1929 dropped to £666 millions in 1930 and to only £461 millions in 1931. At the same time unemployment rose from just over a million in the summer of 1929 to over two and a half million by the end of 1930. Nothing the government did seemed to have any impact on the worsening economic situation, and by the middle of 1931 Britain was in deep financial trouble. The unemployment fund was then borrowing at the rate of £1 million a week to meet the huge bill for benefit, and foreign investors began to withdraw their money from the Bank of England because they feared that Britain was heading towards complete bankruptcy. To make up these losses the government raised loans abroad, but they were only made on condition that the amount spent on unemployment relief should be reduced. The majority of the Labour ministers refused to accept this condition and so the government resigned. It was replaced by a National Coalition Government of all parties, formed specifically to fight the economic battle.

Unfortunately the National Government was no more successful in dealing with the immediate crisis than its predecessors. The financial crash was not averted despite a 10% cut in the rates of unemployment pay, and in September 1931 the pound was devalued to about 70 per cent of its former value. Attempts were then made to steady the situation by raising extra taxes to balance the budget, while help was given to Britain's hard pressed industries. The traditional policy of Free Trade was abandoned in 1932 and import duties of 20% were placed on most foreign goods coming into Britain. At the same time the Ottawa Agreements were signed to promote increased trade between the countries of the British Commonwealth through a mutual lowering of customs duties. It is now generally agreed that none of these measures was very effective. Indeed, by raising taxes and lowering unemployment pay, the government took money out of circulation and almost certainly aggravated the problem of unemployment which reached a peak at the beginning of 1933 with more than three million men out of work. After that there was some improvement. World trade as a whole began to revive from 1933 onwards and Britain began to climb out of the slump. The progress was painfully slow, however, and there were still one and a half million men on the dole as late as 1937. In the long run it was

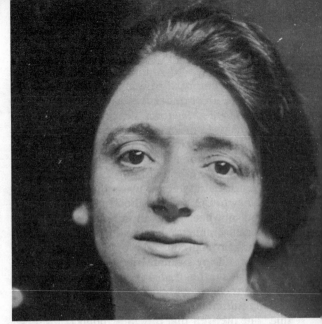

'Red Ellen'. Ellen Wilkinson the fiery Labour M.P. for Jarrow during the slump.

the outbreak of the Second World War more than anything else which put an end to the depression. Only the huge government orders for armaments made the rusty mill wheels turn again and brought work to the shipyards after years of idleness.

The Distressed Areas

As in the 1920's it was again the old staple industries which suffered most in the slump. Cotton, coal, engineering and shipbuilding all fell on even harder times, and the areas in which these industries were carried on became officially classified as 'distressed areas'. The North-East Coast was one of these areas and Jarrow, the Tyneside shipbuilding town, became in the mid-thirties a symbol of the slump. The whole fate of Jarrow was bound up with the fate of Palmers, its shipyard. When Palmers did well, Jarrow prospered. When Palmers closed down, as it did in 1934, the town died because the bulk of its workers had been employed there. The closure was part of the shipbuilding industry's programme of 'rationalization' under which Sir James Lithgow, the Clydeside shipyard owner, and his partners in National Shipbuilding Securities Ltd. bought up small yards in order to close them down and so concentrate what limited amount of shipbuilding business there was in fewer yards. To the shipyard owners and to the government which supported them this made economic good sense, but to the workers of Jarrow it made no sense at all. They had been proud of the yard and proud of their skills and they were angry. In the election of 1935 they registered a protest by returning the fiery left wing Labour politician Ellen Wilkinson as their M.P. and 'Red Ellen' set about bringing the fate of Jarrow to the attention of the nation. In speeches, and in a famous book *The Town That Was Murdered*, she pleaded for special help for her constituents and in 1936 she organized the well known Jarrow Crusade. This march to London by 200 of the town's unemployed was a failure. The government still refused special assistance for the town and when the men got back home they found their dole had been cut because they had not been 'actively seeking work' during the month of the march. Nevertheless this and the other hunger marches of the 1930's did achieve something. They brought the distressed areas to the notice of the more prosperous parts of the country and they boosted the men's morale. Wal Hannington who organized many of these marches said 'The men felt that they were *doing* something, instead of just rotting away'.

Government Aid

Naturally the government felt responsible for the distressed areas and they did do something to help. Training centres were established to teach the unemployed new skills, and some schemes of road and hospital building at the government's expense were started to provide work. Social clubs were also set up and charity organizations were encouraged to go into the areas to do what they could to help. Nowhere near enough money was spent, however, and the best scheme of all, which really did offer some hope for the future, was actually the suggestion of a private individual. Mr. S. A. Sadler Forster, a Middlesbrough accountant

The new town-centre of present day Jarrow which wants very much to lose its image as a slump town.

wrote a letter to *The Times* just before the 1935 election, in which he suggested that the government should open trading estates in the distressed areas to which light industry should be attracted by government grants. This suggestion was taken up and the first estate was opened at Team Valley near Gateshead in 1937. Industrialists were attracted by the low rental of £1 a week for factories, and by 1939, 5000 people were employed there. Considering the numbers out of work this was only a drop in the ocean, but the idea was a good one.

Today Team Valley and the other estates which have been built in the former distressed areas employ 200 000 people and they, and the much larger amounts of public money invested there, have done much to change the north. Jarrow is now a bright modern town trying hard to live down its

The Jarrow Crusade. The unemployed marchers led by Ellen Wilkinson are seen here near Harrogate in Yorkshire.

An unemployed Wigan miner, still without a job in 1939. This picture sums up the hopelessness of the long term unemployed.

disputes, that the desire to hang on to a job at any cost is still strong.

'On the Dole'

Since the efforts of the government had such a small impact on unemployment it was again only the dole which saved the people of towns like Jarrow from starvation, and in the worst years of the slump, between 1931 and 1934, the dole was given even more grudgingly than before. The rate in 1930 for a married man with two children was 30 shillings (£1.50) a week but as a result of the economy cuts imposed in 1931, this was reduced to 27/6d (£1.37½) and to 15 shillings (75p) for a single man. At the same time the hated means test was introduced whereby officials from the local Public Assistance Committee made detailed inquiries about the personal circumstances of every applicant for dole, to see if he had a few pounds in savings, or whether his wife or daughter earned a few shillings a week as a shop assistant. If it was found that he had some other means of support, however slender, then his dole was reduced or even witheld altogether. Many a once proud father found himself in the humiliating position of living off his own children and the means test was bitterly resented. G. K. Chesterton wrote 'It is inhuman. It is horrible. I should not mind the Scribes and Pharisees saying it was inevitable, if only they would say it is horrible'.

Nevertheless despite the reductions and the resentment caused by the whole idea of living on charity, the dole did do what it was intended to do—it kept the unemployed alive. Families had to

slump image but among the people, the scars of the 1930's still show. It is worth remembering, when we criticise men for engaging in restrictive practices and apparently stupid 'who does what?'

Unemployed men learning to dig drainage trenches at a government re-training centre during the slump. Such schemes barely skimmed the surface of the problem of unemployment.

economize on clothes and eat cheap food and there was little left over for toys or holidays or Christmas presents. However, they did manage. Evidence was produced to show that many of the children of the unemployed were suffering from malnutrition in the mid-thirties, and free school milk was introduced for that reason, but in many ways the hardship was not so much physical as mental. After years without work men began to feel useless and rejected, a burden to themselves and to their families. Gradually they lost their pride and their self-respect. Some of the braver ones tried to fight back and there were occasional scuffles with the police, but most of the unemployed became resigned to their fate. They hung around on street corners, perhaps cultivated a small allotment or simply went down to the local men's club to play billiards or table tennis or to gamble for half-pennies at cards and dominoes. After seeing one of these clubs the author, J. B. Priestley, commented sadly 'By the time the North of England is an industrial ruin, we shall be able to beat the world at table tennis'.

Living Standards

Because of the slump it is often assumed that living standards declined in the 1930's, but this is not so. The world-wide depression brought such a sharp drop in prices that those with jobs found a new prosperity. It has been estimated that even families living on the dole were better off than in the twenties, and certainly better off than many lower paid workers with jobs in the period before 1914. Many workers found themselves rehoused following the Greenwood Housing Act of 1930 which ordered local authorities to get on with the job of slum clearance. The author George Orwell saw the effects of this Act when he visited Sheffield in 1936, and he wrote in his diary 'The town is being torn down and rebuilt at an immense speed. Everywhere among the slums are gaps with squalid mounds of bricks where condemned houses have been demolished and on all the outskirts of the town new estates of Corporation houses are going up'. In view of all this, why is the memory of hardship so vivid? Probably the answer lies in the sharp contrast which existed between life in the distressed areas and life elsewhere in Britain. The general prosperity highlighted the drabness and decay in the regions of high unemployment, like the North East, South Wales, Industrial Scotland and Lancashire.

Twentieth Century Britain

This contrast struck J. B. Priestley very forcibly when he travelled through the country in the autumn of 1933 collecting material for his book *English Journey*. In the north he saw the old nineteenth century England of the Industrial Revolution, where work was hard to find and where the towns seemed grey and ugly. By comparison, in the south, he discovered a quite new, twentieth century England of bright modern factories, concrete by-passes and trim suburban housing estates. A land where he saw 'factory girls looking like actresses, greyhound racing and dirt tracks, swimming pools and everything given away for cigarette coupons'. How this prosperous England came to exist alongside the England of unemployment and depression was largely a matter of

Council houses in Sheffield like those George Orwell saw being built in the early 1930's.

Suburban estates being built on the fringes of London in the 1930's. Note how the houses are beginning to sprawl over the open countryside.

markets. The north manufactured the basic export commodities, and demand for these in the 1930's was at its lowest ever. The south and Midlands on the other hand produced motor cars, electrical and household goods, processed food, gramophone records, films and the like, for which there was a growing demand in the home market, particularly in the early thirties because prices were so low. As a result the centres of the new industries, like Coventry and Oxford, Slough, Reading and the suburbs of London, like Hayes and Wembley, thrived. In 1934 when Palmers shipyard closed down and 68% of the workers of Jarrow were on the dole, only 5% were idle in Coventry and Oxford and only 3% in High Wycombe.

Conclusion

Britain in the thirties was thus a country of contrasts. The majority did well. Their wages bought more, and technological progress continued to make their lives easier. Cheaper materials caused another housebuilding boom and this allowed many thousands of families to purchase their own homes in the expanding suburbs, together with

Unemployed workers sing and beg for money in the streets of the West-End of London.

the family car. New cinemas and dance halls provided cheap entertainment, and yet over it all there hung a shadow. Prosperous people in the south could hardly ignore the unemployed miners who shuffled along the London streets singing for a few pence a day or see the hunger marchers arrive from the north without feeling disturbed, and justifiably so. Their prosperity was in many ways artificial. Britain was thriving by selling to herself in the home market, but to live this country needs to export. In 1937 exports were still down at only 83% of the level they had been in 1929 when the slump started, and yet by that time world trade as a whole was picking up. This continuing inability to recapture our old share of the world's markets was a very dangerous omen for the future.

QUESTIONS

1. How was British trade affected by the world wide trade depression, and how did the National Government try to tackle the country's economic problems in 1931 and 1932?
2. Write an account of the effect of the Slump on Jarrow and describe how the people of Jarrow reacted to what happened.
3. What government aid was given to the distressed areas in 1930's?
4. Describe what it was like to live 'on the dole' in that period.
5. Why were the south and Midlands much more prosperous than the north in the 1930's?

17 POST-WAR BRITAIN

The end of the Second World War found Britain both victorious, and bankrupt. Manpower losses had been nothing like as serious as those suffered by Britain in the First World War. Then Britain had lost about 750 000 dead. From 1939 to 1945, however, her losses had been less than half of this— 300 000 killed. The real disaster was financial. In 1945 Britain faced an economic crisis as grave as the Dunkirk military crisis she had faced in 1940.

Wartime Conditions

The people of Britain had of course experienced considerable hardship in the six years of war. Food was strictly rationed, petrol, paint, clothes, furniture etc., all the essential aids to living in fact, were in short supply. Bananas disappeared, not to be seen again until the war was over. Strenuous and immensely successful efforts were made to keep the children of the nation as healthy as possible with special allowances of such items as milk and orange juice. For the first time in our history an adequate and a balanced diet was available for everyone in time of war. Above and beyond that there were only the extras that money could provide from what was known as the black market but, nevertheless, the protection of the next generation from a health point of view, remains a major triumph.

There was even a lighter side to scarcity. The Ministry of Food, set up at the beginning of the war, was always on hand with make-do recipes. One recipe that became a classic was for a Christmas pudding with carrots as a main ingredient. It worked, up to a point. According to supply and availability, people were exhorted to 'eat more potatoes' or 'eat more bread'. Films, the cinema was very important then, showed you such things as how much water should be taken in a bath— not more than five inches (127 mm) was the recommended level.

A staple ingredient of the diet was a yellow powder imported from the United States called dried egg. This could be made into omelettes, scrambled egg, cakes, or as the cynics said, soles for your shoes. One advantage that Britain did have during the war was the availability of the 'lend lease' arrangement with the United States. This arose from the fact that most of our reserves of dollars had been spent by the end of 1940. The United States decided that it would serve her interests to maintain Britain in the fight against Germany, and from the early part of 1941 she leased or lent vital supplies to the United Kingdom,

A food queue in the East End of London. Queues were a common sight in wartime Britain.

and so food imports from the United States could be ferried here past the German submarine menace. At the end of the war lend-lease stopped abruptly and this invaluable aid was no longer available.

The war also helped to shape the powerful feeling that led to sweeping social changes which came after the ending of the war. Rationing, controls, the cry for equal shares and equal sacrifice from all members of the community, rich and poor alike, helped to produce a feeling that such sacrifice should lead to a society in which everyone should have the right to have a decent standard of living, to be shielded from the harsh effects of unemployment and to have the effects of sickness and old age cushioned by social security.

At the height of the war, in 1942, the government had felt it necessary to take these feelings into account by commissioning Sir William Beveridge's 'Report on Social Insurance and Allied Services'. As a young civil servant, William Beveridge had helped to organize the payment of the first old age pension of 1909. Now he proposed an all embracing system of social security. It offered protection for the family 'from the cradle to the grave' against sickness, poverty, unemployment etc., by the provision of pensions, family allowances, free health treatment, vastly improved educational opportunities and all-covering National Insurance. Some far reaching Acts of Parliament were actually passed during war time. The Town and Country Planning Act of 1944 aimed to prevent unplanned

development of our precious but dwindling heritage of open country. Mr. R. A. Butler's Education Act, passed in the same year, provided for the school leaving age to be raised to fifteen and also foreshadowed the creation of a system of education based on secondary modern, secondary technical and secondary grammar schools. 'Secondary education for all' was to be provided. Family Allowances also first appeared in 1945. All these Acts of Parliament were the product of the wartime all-party coalition government. The question to be answered for most people, however, was which political party was most likely to move on enthusiastically towards a full blooded Welfare State as outlined by Beveridge. To many who voted in the 1945 election the answer seemed to be the Labour Party.

The reason for this is not hard to see. Earlier chapters have shown how socialists believed that complete, or near complete, state control of major industries was the way by which unemployment and bad social conditions, poor housing for instance, could be met. It was felt that the other political parties had made little impression on these problems in the interwar years. The Labour Party got its chance to put socialist policies into operation when it won the 1945 parliamentary election with 393 seats to 213 Conservative and allied seats.

The Labour Government 1945–1951

Labour had formed governments earlier, in 1924 and 1929, as we have seen, but never with an overall majority. Hugh Dalton, the Chancellor of the Exchequer, said of the feeling which he and his colleagues shared, that the 'first sensation was of a new society to be built; and we had power to build it. . . . We felt exalted, dedicated, walking on air, walking with destiny'.

Despite crippling financial problems the Labour Government pressed on with its social and economic plans. The principle followed by Labour in its economic policy was that of Nationalization, that is taking over an industry or business so that it could be run by the state for the people. Labour called this the taking over of the commanding heights of industry and the social services. The principle was not a new one. The police, post office and a national education system are earlier examples of state control.

The usual practice in carrying out nationalization was to set up a national board to run each concern as a public corporation, and to announce a 'vesting date' for the board to take control. The first 'vesting date' was for the Bank of England in March 1946. Civil Aviation followed in August 1946 and then coal, cable and wireless on the 1st January 1947. Also in 1947 Acts of Parliament provided for the nationalization of the Railways and

Canals, Electricity and Gas. Railway nationalization had been discussed a hundred years earlier and it has been always contended by socialists that a country's main system of transportation (as railways were then) should not be left in private hands. In fact government control of railways had been steadily increasing throughout the twentieth century, and in this case nationalization was only a logical final step.

In 1949 the Iron and Steel industry was nationalized (it was later de-nationalized by a Conservative government and then renationalized by the first Wilson Labour government). Iron and Steel made a profit, most of the others did not do so at that time, and this helped to leave the impression that nationalization was a system suitable for loss-making concerns which might be considered socially useful, but that it was not something to be applied to profit making industries.

Despite the all embracing appearance of this formidable nationalization programme, 80% of the country's industry remained in private ownership. There was little sign that employees in the new State owned industries felt that they had a greater stake in the country, although miners certainly noticed a real improvement in their working conditions, and the railways at last began a much needed modernization programme, which led to the electrification of some main line routes from 1955. In recent years there have been considerable reductions in services as increased car ownership has made inroads into passenger numbers.

It was the programme of social reform that made a real impact on the individual British citizen. Labour claimed at the General Election that it intended to make provision 'for all our people'. In so doing they vastly extended the work begun by the Liberals in the period 1906–1914 and developed those beginnings into a fully fledged 'Welfare State'.

The aim was to 'provide a shield for every man, woman and child in the country against the ravages of poverty and adversity'. In so doing there was a close link with the ideas contained in the Beveridge report mentioned earlier. The two great Acts of Parliament on which all this hinged were the National Insurance Act of 1946, the work of James Griffiths, and the National Health Act of 1946, pushed through Parliament by the driving force of Aneurin Bevan, the Minister of Health. Both Acts were the work of Welshmen and both came into force in 1948.

National Insurance provided cash benefits for sickness, unemployment, widowhood and retire-

A famous war-time poster.

IG FOR VICTORY

For their sake -

GROW YOUR OWN
VEGETABLES

The Festival of Britain site at South-Bank in 1951. Note the Dome of Discovery on the left, and behind it, the Skylon. Most of the buildings were taken down when the Festival was over, but the Royal Festival Hall on the right of the picture remains as a permanent feature of present day London.

ment, in return for regular payments deducted from a person's weekly earnings. The Act covered everyone, males from 16–65 and females 16–60, not just the specific classes of worker listed by Lloyd George.

The National Assistance Act of 1948 completed the work of sweeping away the remnants of the Poor Law. Cases of hardship now qualified for what have become known as supplementary pensions.

The National Health Service Act set out to provide free medical help for everyone. At the beginning of the scheme drugs, medicines, false teeth and spectacles were provided free of charge. Later, fees for such items were re-introduced. And of course, in one sense, the treatment has to be paid for anyway, in rates and taxation. At the outset there was opposition from the doctors as there had been to Lloyd George in 1911, but Aneurin Bevan refused to be diverted. He battled through a series of stormy meetings with the British Medical Association, spurred on by the need, as he saw it,

to abolish poverty and tragedy as he had seen it in his young days in South Wales.

Finally during this period of feverish activity the Butler Education Act of 1944 was implemented; the school leaving age being raised to fifteen in 1947.

The Financial Crisis

Over everything that the Labour Government did and wished to do, there hung the shadow of the financial crisis which faced the country at the end of the war. Britain's debts were enormous. Much of our valuable overseas investment had been sold to help pay for the war. Nearly half our merchant shipping had been lost and the fearsome problem of the balance of payments remained; we could not export enough to pay for the food and raw material we needed to import, and we lacked dollars to buy what we needed from the United States. Lend-lease was ended abruptly by the United States just seven days after Japan surrendered. The Labour govern-

110

ment had hoped that it would be gradually tapered off. As an alternative a massive loan of dollars had to be negotiated. Again Labour hopes of getting a no-interest loan, as a return perhaps for our effort when fighting alone, were also dashed. In the end, Britain received 4.4 billion dollars, (£1000 million) at two percent, to be repaid by the beginning of the Twenty-first Century.

Hopes that this would plug the gap were doomed. In two years much of this had been spent. This was despite the 'austerity' which Britain followed. The government, guided by Stafford Cripps, the Chancellor of the Exchequer after Hugh Dalton, had to maintain rationing at levels even lower than the wartime rates. Indeed bread was rationed for the first time. Coal was in short supply. Clothes were shabby and soon wore out.

In 1949 the government was forced to reduce the price of our exports by the drastic step of devaluing the pound from 4 dollars to 2 dollars 80 cents. The export drive *did* respond to this. Also fresh American help in the shape of Marshall Aid (General Marshall being the man who organized it) *did* have some effect, although it did not prevent devaluation. By 1950 the country's financial position began to improve, but by 1951 Labour was out of power and the Conservatives took over.

Although Labour had faced grave problems with courage they had become too much linked in people's minds with controls and rationing—in fact the whole business of austerity.

The positive social achievements were soon taken for granted. Politicians of all parties are acutely aware of the short memories of the electorate in such matters.

One splash of colour brought the Labour period of rule to an end. This was the Festival of Britain which was designed to commemorate the Great Exhibition of 1851, to help our exports and to brighten up generally a drab period. There were jokes about the symbol errected at the Festival called the Skylon. It seemed to stand up without any visible means of support. Like Britain said the cynics! But it was well organized and featured a Dome of Discovery and the Royal Festival Hall, the latter being still in evidence on the London South Bank site where the Festival was staged.

The Conservative Fight

One curious feature of Britain during the next few years was the way in which the same problems that had haunted Labour continued to plague the Conservatives. It was also true that their answer to these problems had a distinctly similar look to those of their predecessors.

The Conservatives, in the words of one of their leaders, had come into office with 'a heavy load of promises. We had said we would set the people free, ... the ... Government was pledged in its election manifesto to undo much of the Socialist legislation of the preceeding six years'.

In fact there was little denationalization. Railways and mining remained in public ownership. When money was needed for arms, the Conservatives simply cut the subsidies on food, whereas Labour had put charges back on medical prescriptions. To many people there seemed little difference in their measures. Improvement in our balance of payments seemed to come about only when world trade improved, and Government measures had little direct effect.

Nevertheless, for many British people the later 1950's was the time when they entered the 'affluent society.' The Minister of Housing, Mr. Macmillan, seemed to have the knack of getting houses built quickly. Income tax was lowered, rationing ceased and television sets, motor cars, refrigerators and washing machines became indispensible items in many households. By the middle 1960's nearly 40

Compare this postwar advertisement with present day car advertisements.

For the family whose car is always in use . . .

The Hillman Minx is a car for the whole family to share . . . safe, easily handled in crowded streets . . . fast, roomy and comfortable on a long drive to the coast . . . quietly dignified for an evening in Town. A car that never runs up costs, that always keeps appointments . . . for the family whose car is always in use.

HILLMAN MINX

% of British homes had refrigerators—but there were still millions of homes without a bathroom.

Affluence grew even quicker under Mr. Macmillan's prime ministership in the early 1960's. He himself was moved to remark that the people of Britain had 'never had it so good'.

R. J. Unstead gives a table for the later years of his period of office to show just what affluence meant.

From 1959 to 1964 people's spending on comfort and enjoyment increased as follows:

Beer	+ 14%
Food	+ 21%
Furniture, carpets etc.	+ 25%
Clothing, footwear	+ 39%
Wines, spirits etc.	+ 61%
Radios, electrical etc.	+120%
Cars, motor-cycles	+530%

The last two items are particularly significant. Transistors, and pop records obviously make their contribution to the one, and the general desire of all sections of the population to own a car is reflected in the other.

The affluence was something that the fit and fully employed could gain. The sick, the under-employed and the old age pensioner did not share in the spoils. Nor did the Welfare State and its services.

The country could spend hundreds of millions of pounds on entertainment, tobacco, drink and suchlike, but it did not build a single hospital in the 1950's.

There was another price to pay. The rise in average earnings outpaced the rise in prices throughout the 1950's. At the beginning of the 1960's the fact had to be faced that the balance of payments was running strongly against Britain once more.

The Struggle for Economic Recovery

Britain's membership of the Common Market and the long and sometimes painful struggle towards the establishment of a prices and incomes policy reflect two of the main approaches followed by successive governments in an attempt to correct our adverse trade balance. Membership of the Common market seemed to offer a chance for Britain to share in the trade and prosperity of the wealthy European countries who had signed the Treaty of Rome in 1957. After two applications to join the Market had been blocked by France, Britain was successful at the third attempt and she entered the European Economic Community in 1973. Britain's first ever referendum confirmed this when the British people voted a majority decision in favour of remaining a member in 1975.

In an effort to make our exports more competitive, both Conservative and Labour governments have sought ways of keeping wages at a realistic level whilst endeavouring to modernize our aging and sometimes ailing industries. In 1961, Mr. Macmillan's Conservative government was forced to hold down wages by means of a compulsory 'pay pause'. It had little effect as it operated fully only in public services such as nursing, teaching and the civil service. The year 1964 saw Labour come to power under Mr. Wilson. A Declaration of Intent was produced by the government, management and the main unions aimed at 'a rapid increase in output and real incomes'. A National Plan appeared in 1965. Its target was a balance of trade surplus by 1970. The reality was a devaluation of the pound in 1966. In 1969, the Chancellor of the Exchequer was compelled to report that he considered that 'our competitive power has been damaged by irresponsible industrial action'. In saying this the Chancellor had in fact laid stress on the crippling effects as he saw it of strike action, particularly when such strikes were 'unofficial', that is lacking union backing.

Labour drafted a Bill 'In Place of Strife' designed to deal with this problem. Owing to the lack of support from the unions themselves the Bill has to be abandoned. The Conservatives, back in power in 1970, brought in an 'Industrial Relations Act' hoping that it would get rid of 'unfair practices' by taking action against unofficial strike leaders. The government also wanted all unions to belong to a 'register' and proposed heavy financial penalties for any union that refused to take this step. The Trades Unions Congress complained with some justification that unions were being compelled to have a 'state licence to carry out essential fuctions'. The feeling gained ground that compulsion was not the answer and that a proper pay policy was needed, one that covered prices, and dividends, not one that concentrated on wages alone. Various formulae have been tried. Mr. Heath and the Conservatives operated a scheme that gave everyone pay rises of £1 plus 4% of their existing wage. The Conservatives could not sustain their policies in the face of a miners' strike. Labour, back in power in 1974, had one rather doubtful advantage in its favour in that the very high level of inflation that was running in Britain by 1975 probably scared most sections of the community into accepting a flat rate pay increases of £6 a week as part of an agreement between the government and the trades

Union Congress. A vast loan secured from the International Monetary Fund at the end of 1976 has helped to provide a further breathing space for our hard-pressed economy. As this book went to press the first proposals for a third round of wage limitations were being made. Again, much will depend on the restraint shown by wage-earners in the face of an annual inflation rate of about 16%.

North Sea Oil

Although a successful incomes policy is a vital part of Britain's drive for future prosperity her main long term hopes centre on oil from, the North Sea. Until 1975, Britain produced only a fraction of the oil she needs for running and heating homes, factories and transport. Our oil imports were costing us over 3000 million per annum, most of it coming from the Persian Gulf, Nigeria and Venezuela. In 1975, however Britain actually produced 2 million tonnes of her own oil; about one fiftieth of her requirements only but an encouraging sign. In 1976 Britain started to export oil, about 20 million tonnes in May of that year thus earning useful currency for our critical balance of payments.

By 1980, Britain hopes to be producing all the oil

North sea oil. Britain's hopes of coping with the energy crisis of the 1970's and of righting her balance of payments rest to a considerable extent on the development of her north sea oilfields.

she needs from her oilfields in the North Sea and have some left over for export. We are not sure just how much oil there is under the North Sea but some experts think that there is enough for at least fifty years at our present rate of consumption.

It was in 1959 that Esso and Shell found natural gas in the Netherlands. It was known that the geological nature of the deposits were similar to those of the southern North Sea and investigations began which proved the existence of oil in addition to reserves of natural gas. Soon the exploratory drills of the oil companies were moving further and further north even beyond Orkney and Shetland and by the early 1970's big oil fields were being reported from these areas. The Forties field, 120 miles north of Aberdeen, was struck in October 1970, the Brent field, 120 miles off Shetland, was found in 1971 the Ninian field in 1974.

The oil is obtained by using the type of rig that you can see in the photograph. At the heart of the rig is the drill which pushed down into the sea bed whilst the rig by dropping huge telescopic legs down to the sea bed. The drill consists of a long tube of steel with a tip of steel or diamond teeth which bite into the oil bearing deposits. When the oilmen are sure that there is a substantial field to be worked, a production platform is positioned over the site and the oil is extracted and pumped ashore by means of a pipeline. Britain's North Sea oil is known as a 'light' oil and she will have to sell some of it in order to buy the 'heavy' oil that is needed for lubrication.

Costs are enormous. Rigs can cost up to £25 million, a production platform over three times as much. Pipeline works out at nearly £1 million a kilometre to buy and to lay under the sea bed. Huge loans had to be raised to pay for all this and in addition, as we have seen, Britain has borrowed heavily in recent years against the security of North Sea oil in order to help her balance of payments. So in effect we have already spent some of the money we have yet to receive from our oil.

Then there is another sort of price. The rapid growth of the oil industry has had a considerable effect in Scotland. The high wages paid to the oilmen for their dangerous work in the North Sea have made it difficult to obtain workers for lower paid occupations, such as those in retail trades and the hotel industry. House prices have soared beyond the reach of many. Indeed Aberdeen it is said now resembles the type of town that grew up during the gold rushes of the nineteenth century! There are also the protest of the conservationists concerned about the siting of production areas in former beauty spots, and there are those who claim that the prosperity brought by oil is purely temporary and no answer to long term unemployment.

Several hundred years ago, a Scotsman prophesied that when the 'black water' came to Scotland there would be times of trouble. Events have prove him right. In a wider sense it is to be hoped that Britain's economic expectations arising from the development of her own oil do not prove to be over optimistic.

QUESTIONS

1. a) What developments in wartime Britain helped to explain the social reforms of the Labour Government 1945–1951?
   b) Make a chart showing the main Acts of Parliament passed in these years. Explain the nature of each Act.
2. Why has Britain faced recurring financial crises in the years after the Second World War? What possible solutions are there to this situation?
3. Why did Mr. Macmillan, when he was Prime Minister, feel justified in saying that the British people had 'never had it so good'?
4. Outline the most significant stages in the struggle to achieve an incomes policy.

SECTION 5

Our Own Age

If a stranger visited Britain and heard us complain about high taxes, rising prices and the other day to day grievances we have, he might assume that we were very badly off. Of course, he would be wrong. Despite the fact that everyone would like more money or more holidays or shorter hours, we are, in fact, living in an age when ordinary people have more of the good things in life than at any previous time in our history. We have only to compare our own everyday lives with the lives of people who lived only fifty or sixty years ago to see how far we have progressed, at least in the direction of material comfort and physical well being. For the most part we are better housed, better fed, better educated and healthier than people in Britain have ever been.

Much of this progress has come in the last half century thanks to two recent 'revolutions' which future generations of schoolchildren will no doubt learn about, just as you learn about the Industrial and Agricultural Revolutions. On the one hand there has been a very important social revolution which has raised the living standards of ordinary people tremendously, and on the other there has been a scientific revolution which has done much to make our lives easier and more comfortable. In Section 5 we shall look at some of the features of life in our own age and see just how far our lives have been influenced, not only by the important economic changes which began in the eighteenth century, but by the more recent developments in this present century.

18   IMPROVED STANDARDS OF LIVING

Standards of living in Britain improved throughout the nineteenth century as greater national wealth and vast technical improvements made it possible to supply the needs of the growing population.

The Early Twentieth Century

This improvement was apparent if we look back to the early years of the present century when the average Englishman was certainly better off than he had been a hundred years before. By 1900, for example, cheap cotton goods and the development of a ready-made garment industry had ensured that he was better clothed, and changes in taste and fashion and improved fabrics were making clothes lighter, more hygienic and easier to wear. In the Edwardian period women were freed from the clutter of petticoats that Victorian fashion had decreed they should wear, and waists began to return to a more normal size as the whalebone 'stays' of Victoria's day were cast aside. Clothes also became more practical. The city gentleman's

long frock coat went out of fashion early in the century and women's skirts became shorter and more suited to active city life in the days of the new motor omnibus. Skirts in Edwardian times not only revealed a lady's ankle (always considered very daring) but they also showed two or three inches of the leg above the ankle; a fact which aroused as much critical comment in those days as the mini skirt did in the late 1960's.

The same improvement could be noted in diet. The working class Englishman's diet in 1800 had often consisted of bread, potatoes and oatmeal with meat an occasional luxury. By 1900 refrigeration, imports of canned goods and the great expansion in British farming in the middle of the nineteenth century had brought about a revolution in eating habits. Fresh milk and vegetables from the countryside, New Zealand lamb, Argentine beef and imported cheese and bacon had all found their place on working class tables along with such items as golden syrup and mass produced jams and biscuits. The diet was certainly plainer

Edwardian children playing outside the fineworker's cottages built by Levers at Port Sunlight in Cheshire.

than that which we enjoy today, but it was wholesome and balanced and was an important factor in the improved health standards which were then apparent, at least among the better paid workers.

In housing we can also find similar evidence of progress by the early twentieth century. The 1875 Public Health Act (see page 83) had laid down a new code of building regulations and in the last quarter of the nineteenth century thousands of soundly built 'by-law' houses were erected. Many of these can still be seen in our large cities and in them the better-off working class families could live a decent life. They usually had two or even three bedrooms, a sitting room and living room, a kitchen and a scullery with a copper for washing clothes. Outside in the whitewashed backyard each would have its own separate privy or water closet and perhaps even a few feet of grass and room for a privet hedge and some flowers. Inside, the main rooms would be gas lit and the kitchen would be provided with a large cast iron range for cooking and heating water. Some workers, those fortunate enough to be employed by Lever's Soap Works or Cadbury's chocolate company, would be even better housed because this was the period in which Lord Leverhulme and George Cadbury were completing their model estates at Port Sunlight in Cheshire and Bourneville on the outskirts of Birmingham.

All these features of early twentieth century life were an improvement on much of what had gone before, but we must remember that for people living even in this state of relative comfort life was

harder than it is in our own day. The improved diet we have commented on was by our standards very plain, and Charles Booth pointed out in his famous survey *The Life and Labour of the People of London*, which he compiled between 1886 and 1903, that while many families had enough to eat few had more than enough. Similarly we should also find much of the housing plain and even grim. The tunnel back houses (so called because of their narrow frontage and dark backs) often had no bathrooms and they were usually built in long monotonous rows and opened directly onto the street. For this reason the front room was usually very cold, and this is one reason why it was reserved for 'state' occasions like a family funeral or an unexpected call from the vicar. Most floors in the houses were covered with linoleum, the poor man's carpet, and this also tended to make them cold. Running such a house was also harder work for the woman of the family than running a modern home. Wash day, for example, really was a full day's work, which began about seven in the morning when the copper was filled with water and the

The inside of an early electric iron showing the carbon rods which heated up as the current arced across them.

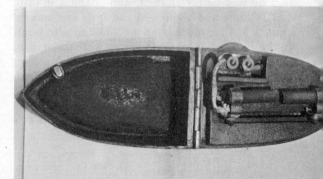

116

fire lit underneath. This would heat up during breakfast and then the clothes would be washed in soap (no 'whiter than white' detergents in those days) and agitated with a 'dolly' or scrubbed on a washboard. They would then be laboriously wrung out through the wooden rollers of a heavy, cast iron mangle and put out to dry. In the evening they were ironed with a heavy flat iron heated on the fire or the gas stove and put on the rails which were suspended from the kitchen ceiling to air. This ended wash day, perhaps twelve hours after it had begun. Small wonder a washing machine and an electric spin dryer are high on the list of requirements for a young bride setting up house these days. Cleaning the house without such gadgets as a vacuum cleaner also added to the difficulties of running a home, and few wives went out to work in those days. This robbed families of the second income which many find so useful today, although it may well have contributed to a more stable home life.

Poverty

What we have looked at so far was life among the better off sections of the working class at the beginning of this century; families in which the father had a trade and earned the average tradesman's wages of about thirty-five shillings a week. There was, however, a large class, usually termed labourers because they had no special skills, who lived well below this standard. These were the poor who lived on wages which were in the region of eighteen or nineteen shillings a week and could afford few of the improvements we have noted. The number of people in this class was considerable.

When washday really was hard work. In this wash-house you can see the soaking and rinsing tub, the dolly tub on the right of the picture and behind it the heavy mangle with its giant wooden rollers.

Booth, in his survey in London, estimated that 30% of the working population was living below the poverty line, and Benjamin Seebohm Rowntree who studied conditions in York in 1901, put the figure even higher, at 43.4% of the wage earning class, the equivalent of 27.84% of the whole population. These statistics were not arrived at very scientifically, but other evidence bears them out. Of the 12 000 men who volunteered to join the army in Manchester in 1899 at the time of the Boer War, 8000 were rejected as completely unfit for military service and, over the ten year period from 1893 to 1903, 36% of all recruits to the British army were not accepted on medical grounds. We can also see the evidence of extreme poverty ourselves, simply by looking at old photographs. Barefoot children in cut down clothes were a common sight on our city streets in the years before the First World War, and the appearance of the Bermondsey school children, who were photographed towards the end of the last century, leaves little doubt that they lived in poverty. (The other photograph, which shows children at the same school in 1959, makes a very interesting comparison). Housing conditions can also be gauged by looking at photographs, like the ones given here which show the Quarry Hill district of Leeds in 1902. The narrow streets of decaying property had already been declared an 'insanitary area' by the Leeds health authorities when the

The Quarry Hill slums in Leeds before 1914.

Children of Snowfield School, London at the end of the 19th. century.

Children of the same school in 1959.

photographs were taken, but it was many years before they, and the thousands of workers' cottages like them in other cities, were removed. With rents at between three and five shillings (15–25 p) a week they were all that many families could afford and, disgusting as they were, they filled a need. Indeed, even houses of this low standard were better than the living conditions of the large number of down and outs with no employment at all who were to be found in every large town. These people, who made up the lowest social class of all, often relied on begging or petty crime for a miserable livelihood and they received little in the way of official help. The one organization which catered successfully for their needs was the Salvation Army, a voluntary body which had been founded in 1878 by William

Modern council houses and flats on the outskirts of Leeds, built since the Second World War.

Booth, a former Methodist preacher from Nottingham.

Booth began his work among the very poor in 1865 when he established a Christian Mission in the slums of Whitechapel in London. He held religious meetings in a large tent and encouraged everyone whatever their background or beliefs to come and hear him preach and join in the singing of hymns. The mission was quite successful but it soon became obvious to Booth and his helpers that preaching was not enough. The poor, crowded into the rotting tenements of Whitechapel, needed more practical help, and gradually the mission turned into a charitable and welfare organization. Booth saw that a really vigorous attack was needed on the lack of religious faith among the poor and upon the wretched social conditions in which they lived and out of this belief there grew his plans for the Salvation Army with its military ranks, its uniform, its discipline and its dedicated desire to serve. By the end of the nineteenth century the Army was doing an enormous amount of good work among the down and outs, the homeless, the ex-prisoners who could not find work and others who were in desperate need. It was also becoming well known through the cheerful street corner prayer meetings which were held in every town and the organization earned widespread affection and respect. In Liverpool's tough dockland, for example, it was an unwritten law that no 'Sally Army' girl should be molested as she went in and out of even the most notorious dock road pubs selling *War Cry*, the Army's magazine, and it was woe betide any seaman or docker who forgot this rule. In our own

Quarry Hill Flats in Leeds, built on the site of the former slum district in the 1930's.

day the Salvation Army is a world-wide organization still doing vast amounts of good work among drug addicts, drop outs and the social misfits of our own day, but perhaps its greatest work was done in the years before the First World War. Then there were so many problems to be tackled and few organizations so willing to help. Certainly there were few which tackled the social evils around them with such vigour and cheerfulness as the ordinary men and women who served in the ranks of General Booth's fine army.

Our Own Day

We have only to look about us to see that much has changed since the early years of the century. New housing estates, bright new schools, well stocked shops and well dressed young people are only a few of the evidences we can see of the social revolution which has taken place in the last fifty years. So many factors have contributed to this progress that it would be impossible to examine all of them in a short chapter such as this, but we can glance at a few of the more important trends.

Undoubtedly one of the most significant developments in this century has been the massive redistribution of wealth which has taken place. Wage levels generally have risen while at the same time heavy taxes placed on the wealthy have helped to finance the welfare services available to us all. Free medical attention, proper schemes of sickness and unemployment pay, outlined in Chapter 16, and a host of other benefits have virtually eliminated poverty, and most working people earn enough to have a little money left over after all the basic household expenses are paid. This can be used to buy the extra comforts and amenities which we have grown used to. Hire purchase is now a generally accepted method of obtaining bigger items, and the boom in credit sales of furniture,

cars, electrical goods and musical instruments which has occurred in the last twenty years or so is an indication of the new prosperity many people have found.

The provision of large numbers of council-built houses at low subsidized rents is another development which has done much to improve standards. A small start in this direction had been made even before 1914, but the really significant developments came after 1919 when local councils began to receive direct financial assistance from the government under the terms of the Addison Housing Act. Large estates of the familiar 'corporation' houses appeared on the outskirts of most cities in the 1920's and 1930's, and massive slum clearance went ahead at the same time. It was in the 1930's for example that the Quarry Hill area of Leeds was cleared and the flats illustrated here erected on the site. Since the end of the war local authorities have continued to provide as many houses as their financial resources have allowed, and in recent years much greater thought has been given to planning. The recently completed estate, shown on the opposite page, is typical of many modern municipal developments, so the photographs on these pages taken together, tell an interesting story of the progress made in housing in just one English city. We must remember too that millions of new private houses have been built in the same period and that many of them are now occupied by working class families who have bought them on a building society mortgage. Home ownership is a thing few ordinary people could have aspired to fifty years ago.

In fact, the list of reasons for our present high standard of living is almost endless. Technical progress, mass production techniques, increased food output as a result of farm mechanization, greater educational opportunities, all these things and many more have played their part. While there are still problems like the serious housing shortage in London, Birmingham, Glasgow and other big cities, it would be a mistake for us to think there is nothing left to be done; but it is nevertheless true that the great mass of British citizens now enjoy a standard of life which is amongst the highest in the world. That this is possible on a small and very overcrowded island is in the long run the greatest benefit that the Industrial Revolution has brought us.

QUESTIONS

1. What evidence was there that living standards were improving at the start of the present century?
2. Which section of the community had been affected only slightly by the improvements? What was life like for these people?
3. We have seen what an ordinary wash day was like fifty years ago. Try to find out about other everyday things in that same period; shopping, travelling to work, taking a bath and so forth. Write a description of some of these things.
4. Compare a tunnel back house with your own home and point out the improvements which have taken place in house design.
5. What sort of things have contributed to the great improvement in standards of living in the last fifty years?

19   LEISURE

In the early nineteenth century working hours were long and leisure a comparatively rare luxury. This was true, not only for factory workers and farm labourers, but also for office workers and shop-keepers and even wealthy industrialists who prided themselves on working the same long hours as their 'hands'. Indeed in the mid-Victorian period work was often regarded as a virtue in itself, and many of the middle classes held firmly to the belief that 'The Devil will find work for idle hands to do'.

In time this attitude changed. More and more people came to realize that it was not possible to enjoy a healthy and useful life without adequate leisure time and, thanks to the Factory Acts and the activities of the trades unions, working hours were reduced in the second half of the nineteenth century. By 1900, an eight hour working day was becoming common in many trades (although hours were still fearfully long in the 'sweated' industries like tailoring) and most industrial premises closed at 2 p.m. on a Saturday. In many industries workers were also given one week's annual holiday, in addition to the Bank holidays at Easter, Whitsun and Christmas which were introduced by Parliament in 1871.

Recently the trend has been towards even shorter hours. The average working week has fallen to about forty hours and most trades now work a five day week which gives employees two full days of leisure. We have certainly come a long way since Samuel Coulson, who, when giving evidence before the Committee on Factory Children's Labour in 1832, agreed that 'The common hours of labour were from six in the morning till half-past eight at night'.

Entertainment

One of the consequences of increased leisure time has been the growth of the modern entertainment industry which has its origins in the music halls of the late Victorian period.

Music halls had existed for many years before this but they began to achieve widespread popularity in the 1870's and 1880's as the demand for more entertainment grew. From that time until the outbreak of the First World War the halls enjoyed a heyday during which the great stars of the period, Little Tich, Florrie Ford, George Robey and many others, toured the country playing to packed houses. Every town at that time had its theatre and even the poorest person could afford a few coppers for a seat in the gallery. Audiences were usually noisy and good humoured, although they had no

Playbill from The Leeds City Varieties Theatre advertising its Christmas show for 1912.

was professional sport played before large crowds of spectators.

In 1850 organized games as we know them hardly existed outside the big public schools but, in 1855, a group of old boys from Harrow founded the Sheffield United Football and Cricket Club. Similar clubs soon followed in other towns, and local football and cricket matches began to attract small crowds of spectators. In 1863 the Football Association was formed to lay down proper rules for the game and the amount of 'soccer' played up and down the country began to increase. To retain their best crowd-pulling players clubs started to pay them in the 1870's and this practice was legalized in 1885 by the F.A. Three years later twelve of the more go ahead clubs who had several professionals on their books, decided to get together in a proper Football League for competition purposes, and in the 1888–1889 season championship matches were played between Accrington, Aston Villa, Blackburn Rovers, Bolton Wanderers, Burnley, Derby County, Everton, Notts County, Preston North End, Stoke, West Bromwich Albion, and Wolverhampton Wanderers. The first league champions were Preston North End who went through the whole season without a single defeat.

The Challenge Cup already existed, having been played for by amateur clubs since 1872, and with regular cup and league matches to watch, football began to draw really large crowds. Only 2000 people watched the first Cup Final in 1872 but over 20 000 turned out to see Preston beat Wolves in the 1889 Final, and in 1901, when Tottenham Hotspur won the Cup by defeating Sheffield United at Crystal Palace, 110 820 spectators saw the game. By that time going to 'the match' on a Saturday afternoon had become a national habit.

First class cricket also emerged as a major spectator sport in the same period. Crowds turned out in the 1870's and 1880's to watch the great W. G. Grace then at the height of his powers, and the first visit from the Australians took place in 1878. Their resounding victory over England in 1882 was followed by the ceremonial burning of some stumps to represent 'the body of English cricket' and the cremated ashes were taken to Australia. These legendary Ashes have been at stake whenever the two countries have played ever since. Professionalism was never quite so readily accepted in cricket as in soccer and a great social distinction was made for many years between 'gentleman' who were amateurs and 'players' who were professionals. There were, nevertheless, a great many professional cricketers who by 1914 were playing in regular championship matches on

hesitation in giving 'the bird' to a bad act, and they were willing to join in the singing of the popular songs of the day. The audience was often kept in order by a chairman who introduced the acts and led the singing, and he needed a ready wit to counter the banter from the 'gods'. A good chairman was as much a part of the show as the performers. This boisterous atmosphere has been brilliantly re-enacted at the Leeds City Varieties, the theatre from which the popular television programme 'The Good Old Days' is broadcast.

In time the music halls were superseded by the cinema, and more recently by radio and television which have brought entertainment into people's own homes. Performers can now expect to play to audiences numbered in millions, and the entertainment business has become a highly organized and complex industry, selling a product which is always in demand now that people have so much free time. One interesting recent trend has been the number of artistes who, having made their names on records or in television, are now going out on tour among the working men's clubs of the north of England where the old music hall tradition is being reborn.

Spectator Sport

Another form of entertainment which also began to develop towards the end of the nineteenth century

121

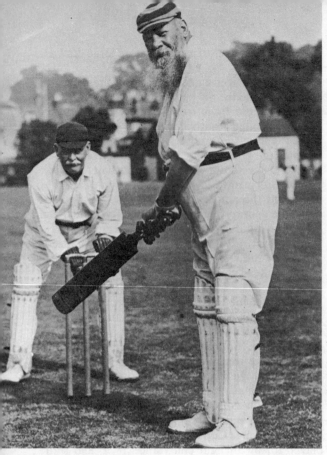

Dr. W. G. Grace in 1913.

Stanley Matthews the 'Wizard of dribble'. The great player is seen here playing for Stoke City.

grounds like Old Trafford, Trent Bridge and Edgbaston, which are still county cricket headquarters. When the First World War broke out spectator sport was already part of the British way of life.

Crowds at big sporting occasions probably reached their peak in the 1930's when cricketers like Jack Hobbs, Wally Hammond and the great Australian batsman Don Bradman were in their prime, and when Stanley Matthews and Tommy Lawton were thrilling crowds with their football skill. In the social conditions of the slump, an afternoon at the local football stadium was the only real excitement in an otherwise drab week and football enthusiasm reached fever pitch in areas of high unemployment like South Lancashire and the North East. Since that time new attractions and greater prosperity have tended to reduce the numbers of regular spectators, and cricket has been particularly badly hit by this trend. Big occasions, the Cup Final, a closely fought Test Match or a major boxing or rugby fixture will still bring out the crowds however. England's World Cup win at Wembley in 1966 was watched by thousands on the ground and millions through television. Sport remains a major British interest.

Leisure Activities

One reason for the recent decline in the size of football and cricket crowds is the simple fact that people now have a great many other things to do. This enormous increase in the variety of leisure pursuits has been particularly noticeable since the end of the Second World War.

People did enjoy all sorts of hobbies and sports before this, of course, and there was a big 'out of doors' movement in the 1920's and 1930's when cycling and hiking were very popular. This movement out of the towns and into the countryside was encouraged by the spread of local bus services and by the establishment of the Youth Hostels Association in 1930, but it did not reach the sort of proportions we know in our own day. Many people seldom escaped from the immediate surroundings of their own town, and lack of money denied them the opportunity of following a variety of interests.

Increasing prosperity since about 1950 has changed all this. Thousands now get out of the towns each weekend into the countryside in private cars, and many pastimes which were once regarded as the preserve of the well-off have become available to a new public. For example, many people now spend their weekends sailing in plywood racing dinghies like the Enterprise and the Mirror which have done so much to popularize the sport, while others go water skiing or skin diving. Rock climbing has become extremely popular in recent years and an increasing number of people are turning to expensive hobbies like photography which they can now afford. Interest in the arts has also increased and local authorities have done a great deal to encourage this by providing evening classes in painting, music, pottery making and so forth and by opening municipal art galleries and theatres. In fact the facilities for leisure have never been greater and they were being added to all the time. The recently opened Billingham Forum on Teesside, with its theatre, restaurant, swimming pool, ice rink and gymnasium is a fine example of a modern leisure centre provided by a local authority and no doubt such centres will multiply as the demand for them grows.

The Daily Mirror dinghy, one of the most successful small boats ever designed. Many thousands of these sailing craft are now in use in different parts of the world.

The Press

The reduction in working hours in the late nineteenth century coincided with the spread of popular elementary education. As a result working men began to read more, both for entertainment and self improvement. This led to a great increase in the number of night schools and free libraries in that period, and to a revolution in the press.

The main agent of this revolution was Alfred Harmsworth, later Lord Northcliffe. He was one of the first to realize that the rather staid and stately newspapers of his day with their long unrelieved columns of print, did not appeal to the newly educated workers emerging from Forster's elementary schools. What they needed was a paper which was bright, easy to read, with

The swimming pool in the Billingham Forum, one of the many facilities available at this fine Teesside Sports Centre.

plenty of headlines and short paragraphs and interesting features. Harmsworth's first paper, a weekly called *Answers to Correspondents* was published in 1888 and owed a lot to George Newnes' *Tit-Bits* which had first appeared in 1880. Harmsworth's drive soon pushed the paper up to a circulation of 250 000 and he was able to put out four other popular 'pulp' magazines which made him a great deal of money. One of these was *Comic Cuts* a paper which brought working class children rather less elevated entertainment than the *Boys Own Paper* which was then very popular in middle class homes.

The financial success of his magazines enabled Harmsworth to move into the field of daily papers which were his real interest, and in 1896 he began to publish the *Daily Mail*. This paper with its rather snappy, sensational style (by the standards of those days) cost a halfpenny, half the price of most other papers at the time, and it was an immediate success. Within three years the *Dail Mail* was selling over 500 000 copies a day and advertisers were naturally attracted by such mass circulation. The other newspapers quickly found themselves engaged in a bitter battle for survival against the *Daily Mail* and its imitators like the *Daily Express*, founded by C. A. Pearson in 1900. Not all of them survived, and even *The Times*, for generations Britain's most famous and highly regarded paper, found itself in difficulties and had to be rescued by Harmsworth himself who bought it in 1907. He wisely decided not to offend *The Times'* old readers by making too many changes in the paper but all the newspapers of the time were affected in some

A page from Comic Cuts *in 1900.*

and still have, enormous influence on public opinion and it is well to remember this when reading a popular newspaper. Most papers have a bias in favour of one political party or another and tend to reflect the views of their owners on important issues. The campaign in the *Daily Express* against Britain's entry into the Common Market is one example of this.

Conclusion

Fifty years ago music halls and the public houses were the main centres of popular entertainment and people had far less time than they have now for hobbies and amusement. Drunkeness in public was then a common sight and temperance reformers were fearful that in future greater leisure would simply bring more excessive drinking and a further decline in morals.

This, of course, has not happened. The English pub is still a popular institution but it is by no means the only haven for people with plenty of free time. Instead greater leisure, coupled with better education and higher wages, has allowed people to widen their interests and live much fuller lives. The last thirty years has seen an increasing interest in music

The front page of the Daily Mirror, *1912.*

way by Harmsworth's revolution. Some ceased publication altogether, others rode out the storm by themselves becoming more popular, and from that time onwards the press became divided into two fairly distinct parts. On the one hand were the popular papers like the *Daily Mail* and Harmsworth's *Daily Mirror* which he started in 1904, and on the other, with much smaller circulations, the more serious publications like the *Daily Telegraph*, the *Guardian* and *The Times*. Power in Fleet Street itself passed into the hands of a relatively few successful newspaper owners of whom Harmsworth was the foremost.

The chief fault of the new popular press was its tendency to ignore really important issues which were dull, in order to concentrate on sensational trivialities, society scandals and the like which were good for sales. As a result of what Harmsworth had achieved the press certainly became less interested in informing its readers, and much more concerned to entertain them. Another disturbing tendency was the slanting of news to fit in with the ideas of the handful of newspaper owners. Through mass circulation these men had,

and the arts, a greater number of people participating in sports and hobbies of all kinds and an enormous increase in the numbers going abroad each year for their holidays. It has also seen a growing number of people attending evening classes and weekend courses and has brought an interesting change in our schools. Clubs for sports and hobbies, trips abroad, mountaineering and sailing expeditions and all the other out of class activities which go on in most secondary schools are really education for leisure; activities provided in school in the hope that when pupils leave they will know how to use their abundant free time in the most satisfying and enjoyable ways.

QUESTIONS

1. See if the cinema or bingo hall in your district was once a music hall and find out what you can about it.
2. Describe the development of football and cricket as spectator sports.
3. Try and find out what you can about the history of your local league football club or your own county cricket club and write a short account of its development.
4. Make a list of the leisure time activities available in your school and in your own district. Find out how many of them are new interests.
5. Describe the emergence of the popular press under Harmsworth in the late nineteenth century. If you have a local newspaper, find out who owns it and whether it has any political bias.
6. Compare a popular daily paper like the *Mail* or the *Mirror* with one of the more serious papers such as the *Telegraph* or *Guardian* and write down any differences you notice between them.

20 SCIENCE AND TECHNOLOGY

In Chapter 14 we saw that many of the forces which have done so much to create the world of our own day were already making themselves felt in what the historian, R. C. K. Ensor, has called the 'seething and teeming years of the Edwardian era. There were new ideas in politics at that time and a new sense of the need for social justice and reform. There were new attitudes towards society and particularly to the place women should occupy in it. Above all there were important new discoveries in science and technology which have since transformed the world. In this chapter we shall examine this twentieth century technological revolution and look at some of its more important consequences.

Scientific Progress

Science, of course, is at the basis of all the more important technical developments of the last fifty or sixty years and the great changes which have taken place are really a reflection of the enormous increase in scientific knowledge. This has been apparent in every field. Physics, chemistry, biology, in fact all the major sciences, have advanced at a remarkable rate since the closing years of the nineteenth century, and whole new sciences like nuclear physics have emerged to pursue more and more specialized lines of inquiry.

At the same time the relationship between science and industry has become much closer. We now have huge science based industries such as electronics in which the laboratory is as important as the production line, and this is something new. The great mechanical engineers of the first Industrial Revolution used science, but very much at second hand. Watt's steam engine was based on a scientific principle which had been known to the Greeks centuries before, but Watt and his contemporaries worked largely by trial and error, doing their own research the hard way. Trevethick's narrow escapes from death on a number of occasions when his high pressure steam engine boilers burst, is just one example of this. Today, in what has been termed the Second Industrial Revolution, every major industry employs its own team of professional scientists who are constantly at work applying their own specialist scientific skills to practical industrial problems. This process, which was beginning towards the end of the nineteenth century in the great German chemical industry and in the infant electrical industry, has been responsible for most recent technological advances. We live in an age of applied science.

The Motor Car

In a short chapter like this it would be impossible to look at all the different ways in which science has affected our everyday lives. We should simply end up with a long catalogue of inventions. We can glance at one or two of the more important developments, however, and perhaps the one with the most far reaching social and economic consequences has been the growth of motor transport.

The internal combustion engine, as we have seen, was invented in Germany towards the end of the nineteenth century, and it was there that the first motor cars were developed. Their use soon spread to the other leading industrial nations and by 1914 the motor car, the motor bus and the motor lorry were familiar sights in Britain, France, Germany and the United States. It was in the 1920's that the real impact of motor transport began to be felt. The bus and the lorry made inroads into the transport monopoly which the railways had enjoyed for so long, and new manufacturing techniques turned the car from a luxury into a more commonplace means of conveyance.

The architect of this particular transformation was Henry Ford, who built his first car in America in 1893 and founded the Ford Motor Company ten years later. In 1908 Ford began to produce his famous Model T, the 'Tin Lizzie' which was the first popular car. The Model T was designed to be

The famous Tin Lizzie. A 1923 version of the Model T Ford.

strong enough for the rutted roads of rural America and was cheap and reliable. It was far from beautiful but it sold in great numbers, and, in order to keep up with demand and keep the price down, Ford began to pioneer his mass production methods in 1913. He is once reputed to have said 'My customers can have any colour car they like, so long as it's black' and this was the basis of his production ideas. He used machines to produce standardized parts of the Model T, and had them put together on an assembly line by semi-skilled labour. At the end of the line there emerged a highly sophisticated piece of machinery, for that is what a motor car is, produced quickly and cheaply by men who knew little beyond their own particular assembly line job. This revolution in manufacturing techniques

A modern assembly line turning out Ford motor cars. This method of producing cars was pioneered by Henry Ford himself before the First World War.

A Vickers Vimy. It was a Vimy that Alcock and Brown used to cross the Atlantic in 1919 and many were later used as civilian airliners in the 1920's.

allowed Ford to produce fifteen million Model T's by 1927 and it was copied all over the world. The multitude of small motor manufacturers which had sprung up in the early 1900's dwindled to a few giant firms in each country who produced cars by Ford's methods. In Britain, as we saw in Chapter 15, Herbert Austin and William Morris were the most successful in adopting this American manufacturing technique, and all the major motor companies in the world now use it. As a result the car for the masses, the early dream of men like Ford and Austin, is now a reality. The private car used for both business and pleasure has brought people a freedom of movement which, in A. J. P. Taylor's words, was 'previously known only to the Gods'. By replacing the horse with the mass produced tractor, the internal combustion engine has also removed much of the drudgery from farming and has had an important impact on food production.

Flying

It is a sad fact that one of the chief causes of scientific advance in this century has been war or the fear of war. The search for ever more destructive weapons has led to considerable progress in all sorts of fields, and this is nowhere more apparent than in aviation. Only a little over ten years after the Wright brothers' historic 'hop' of 284 yards at Kitty Hawk, North Carolina in 1903, aeroplanes were fighting in the skies over the Western Front and were carrying lethal loads of bombs to drop on enemy targets. These early bombers, like the *Vickers Vimy*, which Alcock and Brown used to cross the Atlantic for the first time in 1919, were later employed to pioneer the air routes of the

A model of a Handley Page HP42 airliner of 1930. You can see how these civilian planes developed from the First World War bombers like the Vimy.

A German V2 rocket bomb and trailer. This one is being shipped to Australia after the war to be used as a war memorial in Canberra. The rocket was 14.9 m in length and 2.9 m in width.

both military and civilian, and the Anglo-French *Concorde* was designed to carry its passengers back and forth across the Atlantic at speeds faster than sound. This sort of progress in little more than half a century since the canvas and wire 'kites' of the Edwardian days sums up the pace of change in our own age.

Electricity

Flying has had a relatively limited effect on everyday life and, after the motor car, the technical development which has had the greatest impact has probably been electricity. Here again the result has been an increase in freedom from drudgery. Electric light has replaced candles and oil lamps, electric heat has become available at the flick of a switch and electric appliances like cookers, washing machines and vacuum cleaners have greatly eased the burden of housework. Electricity has also had an impact on transport (though probably less now than in the twenties—the hey-day of the tram) and it now powers many of the factories which mass produce the goods we see all around us. It has, in addition, made possible one other very important aspect of the technological revolution, mass communications by radio and television.

world. From them were developed the early civil air liners like the beautiful H.P. 42 Hannibal class biplanes of Imperial Airways.

In the Second World War progress was even more rapid than in the First, and included improvements to aircraft design and also to navigational aids, ground to air radio communications and so forth. The war also encouraged intensive research into rocket propulsion in Germany and the manufacture of the V1 and V2 rocket bombs and it saw the completion of Frank Whittle's work on jet propulsion in Britain. Since the war, jet engines have been used increasingly for all types of aeroplanes,

Radio and Television

The pioneer work on wireless in this country was carried out by the Italian scientist Guglielmo Marconi who came to Britain in 1896 to work at the Post Office laboratories in London. Within nine months of his arrival Marconi had broadcast messages in morse code over a distance of 12.8 km and in 1901 he successfully picked up a message

The Anglo-French Concorde supersonic jet, with its 'droop-snoot' nose lowered to allow the pilot better visibility.

In the 1920's and 1930's electric tramcars like these were the chief means of public transport in our cities.

broadcast from Cornwall on his apparatus set up at St. Johns, Newfoundland, 3200 km across the Atlantic. Radio sets were installed in many ships from that time onwards and wireless played an important role in the First World War. By 1918 it was theoretically possible to broadcast not only morse code messages but also speech, and the first public broadcasting station in the world was opened in Pittsburg in the United States in 1920. In Britain the Postmaster General had repeatedly refused requests from amateurs for broadcasting licences because he feared that they would interfere with normal telegraph services, but after the success of the American experiment he agreed to allow the Marconi company fifteen minutes a week to broadcast music and news. This time allowance was soon extended, and the Marconi station with its call sign of 2LO quickly became famous. Shortly afterwards it was decided to place all broadcasting in Britain under one company's control and the British Broadcasting Company was founded and began its transmissions in November 1922. In 1927 the company received a Royal Charter and became the British Broadcasting Corporation with new headquarters opened shortly afterwards at Broadcasting House. From 1927 onwards sound broadcasting was entirely in the hands of this public corporation until it was challenged by the shortlived 'pirate' radio stations, like Radio Caroline in the mid-sixties. More recently, local commercial stations, such as Radio London, have been allowed to operate alongside the B.B.C. From the beginning broadcasting was a great success and by the early thirties a radio set was to be found in almost every home.

At the time of the establishment of the B.B.C. experiments were already taking place in the field of television. The leading pioneer in Britain was the Scottish scientist, John Logie Baird, but in fact his particular method of transmitting pictures was not the one eventualy chosen as the standard television system. It was Baird's work; however, which first attracted the attention of the B.B.C. and, as such, he was largely responsible for the establishment of the B.B.C. television service which began transmissions from studios at Alexandra Palace in 1936.

A family watching an early television set in 1938. Programmes from Alexandra Palace could only be picked up in the London area. Television for the rest of the country did not appear until after 1945.

Mary Pickford, the 'World's sweetheart' and uncrowned Queen of Hollywood in the 1920's.

The Cinema

One important form of mass communication and entertainment which was well established even before the spread of wireless in the late 1920's, was the motion picture. Movies were being made even before the First World War and, during the war itself, when the European film industry almost came to a standstill, Hollywood became established as the world's film capital. The sunshine of California made outdoor filming possible all the year round, and 'two reelers' were turned out at a fantastic rate in the war years. The same period brought such masterpieces as D. W. Griffith's *The Birth of a Nation* and saw the cinema become established as big business. At the end of 1915 Charles Chaplin was able to demand, and receive, a contract from the Mutual Film Company which guaranteed him 10 000 dollars a week for fifty-two weeks.

Early T.V. sets were expensive and reception was at first confined to the London area. As a result it was not until after 1945 that television began to attract wider audiences. The establishment of the Independent Television Authority in 1954 and the growth of commercial stations offering an alternative to the B.B.C. programmes did much to encourage the spread of T.V. in the fifties, and today it is as common a form of entertainment as radio was in the thirties. The introduction of a second B.B.C. channel and colour transmissions, has, in more recent years, widened the choice of programmes still further, and with four different radio channels to choose from as well as local radio stations and the new commercial stations broadcasting now caters for the widest possible range of interests.

Throughout the 1920's and 1930's cinema audiences grew. The motion picture industry provided cheap escapism and second-hand thrills which meant a great deal to ordinary people in the years of depression, and studios used publicity to the full to build up the image of their 'stars'. All the world accepted Mary Pickford as its sweetheart in the 1920's, and in the 1930's every shopgirl dreamed of looking and behaving like the legendary Greta Garbo who is still regarded by many experts as the greatest of all film actresses. Films reached a peak of popularity during the Second World War, and one American exhibitor said at that time 'You can open a can of sardines and there's a line waiting to get in'. But then cinema-going began to decline. In Britain the spread of television in the 1950's cut into the mass audiences who had once flocked to 'the pictures', and many cinemas closed down. The film industry fought back with bigger and often better films which were shown to a smaller but more discerning audience. Cynics would say that the popular rubbish once produced by the film industry is now put out instead by the television companies. As Alfred Hitchcock, the director of such films as *North by North West* and *Psycho* said, 'No one will go and watch a bad film at the cinema when they can watch a bad film at home'.

Greta Garbo, the film star of the 1930's who is still a legend today.

Plastics and Man-made Fibres

One scientific revolution of recent years which touches our ordinary lives every day has been the introduction of cheap synthetic materials such as plastics and man-made fibres. These products, with which we are so familiar, are manufactured by one

ICI Wilton near Redcar, Yorkshire where large quantities of Terylene are manufactured.

of the most obviously science based industries, the modern chemical industry.

Chemicals have, of course, been important since the very early days of the Industrial Revolution and the chemical industry expanded rapidly in the late eighteenth and early nineteenth centuries to satisfy the demand for chemicals from the textile trade, from agriculture and from the other users of chemical products. In the late nineteenth century the industry took great strides forward, especially in Germany, and new dyes and explosives and bakelite and celluloid, the first two plastics, were being manufactured before 1914. Rayon was being produced in Britain by Courtaulds before the First World War and in the 1930's new materials such as cellophane went into the shops.

The most rapid strides have been made since the end of the Second World War, however. Nylon, invented by the American firm of Du Pont, was manufactured in England after 1940 for parachutes and then for stockings and clothing after the end of the war in 1945. Terylene, invented by two British scientists Whinfield and Dixon, went into full scale production at a new plant opened by Imperial Chemical Industries (ICI) at Wilton near Middlesbrough in 1955 and since the late fifties another group of man-made fibres, the polyacrylic group, which includes such materials as Acrilan and Orlon, has been developed and put into everyday use. These materials and a wide range of plastics now used for everything from television sets to toys and knives and forks are often superior to the traditional materials they have replaced and are cheap to produce. For these reasons they have done much

to promote the better standards of living we noted in Chapter 18.

Most of the synthetic materials we have talked about are by-products of coal or petrol and the modern chemical industry is usually situated near the coal fields and refineries. This has been a very important development for areas like Teesside which is now a huge petro-chemical centre with refineries and ICI chemical plants bringing prosperity to an area formerly too dependent on older industries like coal mining and iron.

Electronics

The most recent technological advance has been the development of an electronics industry. Electronics is basically a branch of physics concerned with the minute particles of an atom called electrons, and its practical application has chiefly been in the field of communications and computers. In both cases the industrial application of electronics grew as a result of the war and the development of radar and simple computors for gun aiming. Since 1945 research has been intensive, especially in the United States, and electronics have played a major part in the American space programme and such fields as communications satellites. Computers are also being used increasingly by industry and business, where their ability to store information and do rapid calculations is of immense value. In the future, automated factories controlled by computers will come to replace manually operated plants and so free human beings from much dull routine work.

The new nuclear power station built at Hartlepool on the North East coast.

Conclusion

The increased use of computers and a much greater reliance on electricity produced from nuclear power are certainly trends which lie in the future, but forecasting in this age of rapid scientific advance is very difficult. It is hard to imagine what the world will be like ten or twenty years from now. What we can do, however, is to look back and see what the technological revolution has achieved so far.

It has certainly made the world a more dangerous place to live in. The development of nuclear weapons has placed in man's hands for the first time in history the means by which he can destroy himself and all other life on this planet. This places an enormous burden on the statesmen of the world who are trying to keep the peace. Technology has also created other rather more subtle dangers. It was obvious at quite an early stage that the new means of mass communication had an enormous impact on people's minds. The world wide grief in 1926 at the premature death of Rudolph Valentino, the great silent screen 'lover', gave a lurid illustration of the power of films. There were scenes of mass hysteria at his funeral and women were said to have committed suicide when they heard the news of his death. A much more sinister sign of the effect of radio was Hitler's success in spreading his ideas of violence and hate through wireless broadcasts to the German people in the 1930's, and most of the other dictators, Stalin, Mussolini and Franco for

The mushroom cloud that could destroy the world. But nuclear power can be, and is, harnessed successfully to man's domestic needs.

132

example, used radio and film propaganda to good effect. We, ourselves, are constantly being bombarded with advertising matter over the air to persuade us to buy this product or adopt that fashion and such constant pressure is hard to resist. We are so often influenced by the mass opinion-makers that some people fear that we will lose all our individuality and become part of what one critic has called the great unthinking 'admass'. This is perhaps an over pessimistic view, but technological progress does bring its own dangers and we must guard against them.

Progress has also brought very obvious benefits, however. The scientific exploitation of natural resources and the development of methods of mass production have made the industrial nations of the world very wealthy, and this wealth has made possible the high living standards and abundant leisure time we all enjoy. Since the art of medicine has advanced very rapidly in the same period, science has also made it possible for us to live longer and more healthy lives in which to appreciate its benefits. We shall examine this particular aspect of scientific progress in the next chapter.

QUESTIONS

1. In what ways has the development of electricity eased your own life at home and outside it?
2. Using the sections in this chapter as a basis and any additional material you can find in reference books in your library, write a brief history of the development of the following;
   a) The motor car
   b) Flying
   c) The film industry
   d) Radio and television in Britian.
3. What dangers has technical progress brought in recent years? Do you think the benefits of scientific advance outweigh these disadvantages? Give your reasons.

21   THE ADVANCE OF MEDICINE

Earlier chapters have emphasized how the National Health Service, as part of the Welfare State, gives protection against illness. Every British citizen is entitled to receive the benefit of medical treatment under its auspices. It is therefore worth remembering that these benefits are only of value because of the great advances made in medical knowledge during the period covered by this book.

People can sometimes be pre-occupied by a belief in the value of returning to the 'good old days'. Any study of history should put one on guard against such a statement. One would need to make a great mental adjustment in medical matters to go back to the era of blood letting as a major cure for most ailments, to amputation carried out without the aid of anaesthetics and to the dreadful suppuration or decay of the flesh that often set in after an operation. Speed was the only means whereby a surgeon could reduce the period of pain. One nineteenth century surgeon could amputate a leg in under a minute, but post-operative shock and infection usually took their toll after any major operation. The 'bench' in the photograph of the operating theatre at old St. Thomas's Hospital will give some idea of the grim conditions that prevailed in surgery (p. 137).

Medical treatment at any level was in fact of doubtful value. It has been argued that the lack of provision of medical treatment for the mass of the population was in itself no great disaster, as it was not until the twentieth century that such treatment was of definite value. This is rather extreme, as some very important steps had been taken in the fight against pain and disease before the present century. But it is important to remember that for many people, a doctor was out of reach either physically because there was not one living in their vicinity, or financially because the cost of medical treatment was too high when set against an average wage rate.

Some Important Discoveries

British doctors played a leading part in the development of modern medicine. Edward Jenner, a Gloucestershire doctor, carried out a successful immunization of the human body against smallpox in 1796. He did not in fact discover the principle. In the East people were inoculated with a mild form of smallpox in order to protect them from the danger of a serious attack. Lady Mary Montague went to Turkey in 1717 and had her son inoculated then. She popularised the process in England in 1721 and her daughter Mary was among the first to be treated. Also an English farmer, Robert Jesty, had vaccinated his children with cowpox in 1774, over twenty years before Jenner carried out his experiments. Jenner based his technique on the observation that milkmaids who caught a disease called cowpox from the sores on a cow did not catch smallpox. He managed to isolate a substance from cowpox sores on the hands of a dairymaid called Sarah Nelnes, and he then injected this substance into a boy to whom he later gave smallpox vaccine. The boy did not catch smallpox and it was clear that the cowpox had acted as a successful deterrent. The word vaccination was used to describe the technique, the word 'vacca' being the Latin word for a cow.

Jenner's ideas were opposed by other doctors, but later he received a large award (£30 000) from Parliament. Compulsory vaccination against smallpox banished this disfiguring and sometimes fatal disease.

The harrowing pain associated with surgery was a problem that taxed the minds of a number of scientists and doctors. Sir Humphrey Davy showed how the gas nitrous oxide, 'laughing gas', could be used to put people to sleep without there being harmful after effects. Other men including an American, William Morton, experimented with

'Laughing gas'. George Cruickshank's cartoon on the effects of the first anaesthetics.

ether sprinkled on to a handkerchief. Then in 1847 James Simpson, a young Scottish doctor, successfully used chloroform as an anaesthetic. Actually he and some of his friends had experimented in breathing various other gases before the occasion on which they used chloroform, and ended up lying unconcious on the floor. Again there was resistance to the use of a new technique. It was said to be unmanly. A clergyman said that it was a device of Satan designed to 'rob God of the deep, earnest cries which arise in time of troubles for help'. Simpson countered cleverly by quoting the Bible. When God made Eve from Adam, he pointed out, Adam was put into a deep sleep by God. But gradually anaesthesia became an accepted part of surgery, particularly when Queen Victoria used it to ease the birth of one of her children, Prince Leopold.

However, nearly half of the patients who underwent surgery still died of post-operation infection. As early as 1700, however, a Dutchman, Van Leewenhoek, had constructed microscopes which showed millions of tiny creatures in water and other

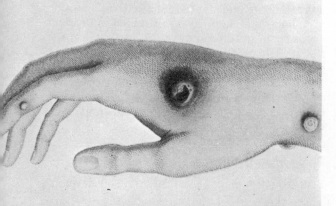

The hand of Sarah Nelmes. Sarah Nelmes was infected with cowpox in 1796. Edward Jenner took lymph from the pustule shown, for his first vaccination.

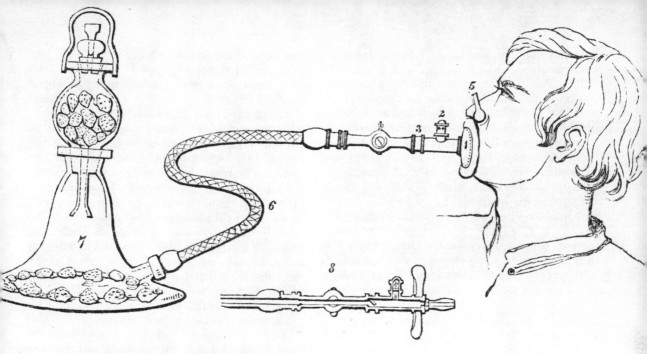

An early anaesthetic apparatus used in operations in 1847 and described as follows: The New Means For Rendering Surgical Operations Painless

1. Pad for mouth, to be held by the operator. 2. Horizontal valve for the escape of expired air. 3. Vertical flap valve. 4. Stop-cock.
5. Nasal spring. 6. Elastic tube. 7. Glass vessel, with a smaller one having pieces of sponge saturated with ether, and having a small perforated stopper, to be opened when the apparatus is in use. 8. Sectional view of the pad, showing the mouth-piece.

liquids. These "little beasties', as Van Leewenhoek called them, were also seen over 150 years later by Louis Pasteur, a French Chemist. He decided that what he called 'germs' were responsible for turning milk sour and for making meat go bad. In 1865 a Glasgow surgeon, Joseph Lister came to the conclusion that it was these germs that were infecting wounds. His answer was to soak all dressings in carbolic acid. At first his solution of carbolic acid was too strong and burning resulted. Lister toned down the strength of the acid by using water and oil, and sprayed the solution on to the dressings and the surrounding area of the operating theatre. He also made certain that his instruments were boiled and that his hands and clothing and those of his assistants were absolutely clean or sterilized.

Along with these developments came better standards of nursing. After her work in the Crimean War, Florence Nightingale devoted the rest of her life to the improvement of nursing and hospital standards.

These were major steps forward, but it is in the present century that the full benefits of these advances have been felt. The inscription which appears on a gravestone in Wales:

In Loving Memory of the children of Edward and Sarah Williams late of Ty-coch, Sychtyn

Joseph Lister, the surgeon and scientists who pioneered the use of antiseptics.

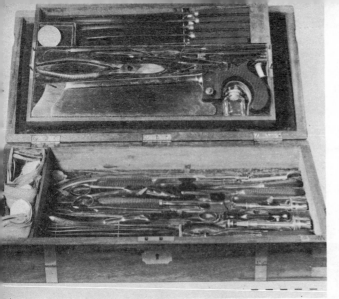

Set of 19th century surgical instruments. The saw was used to
amputate limbs, hence the common use of the name 'saw-bones'
to describe a doctor.

Annie J., died March 16th 1892 aged 5 years
Charles H., died March 21st 1892 aged 2 years
Sarah E., died March 23rd 1892 aged 10 years
Also Mary Williams, mother of the above Sarah
   Williams, died March 24th 1892 aged 65 years
Mary E., died March 28th 1892 aged 8 years
Rose M., died March 30th 1892 aged 3 years
David L., died April 4th 1892 aged 6 years:
and the mortality rate for the East End of London
quoted in Chapter 14, will remind you again that
only 60 years ago life expectancy was still very short
for many people. A vital modern development has
been the vast increase in the range of protection
offered by vaccination and inoculation. Diseases

that once could spell death are now tamed. Dip-
theria, whooping cough, scarlet fever, poliomylitis,
even measles can now be warded off by the appropriate vaccine.

The hand of the doctor has also been strengthened by the addition of a whole range of drugs designed to fight general infection. In 1929 Dr. Fleming
noticed that some bacteria he had in his laboratory
had been destroyed by a mould he called penicillin.
It took ten years of hard work, however, before
other scientists were able to produce penicillin in
a form that could be applied to human beings, but
from the early days of the second World War
penicillin has been available to attack and destroy
many, though not all, forms of bacteria. Doctors
can enlist the aid of a number of other anti-biotics
to fight bacteria, the principle being that they are
living substances that feed on the bacteria.

There are also the sulphanilamides. In 1938 May
& Baker produced M & B 693, useful against
pneumonia, and again, there was a vast development in this field and there are now literally
thousands of these preparations available.

Hospitals and Doctors

The advance of medical knowledge by itself is no
guarantee of a healthy population. There is the
need to have a fully adequate hospital system and
enough qualified nurses and doctors to man them
and to provide a family doctor service.

At the beginning of the eighteenth century there
were three hospitals only, St. Bartholomews, St.
Thomas's and the Bethlehem Hospital for the
mentally ill, all in London. One of the encouraging

A ward in the Hampstead Smallpox Hospital, 1870

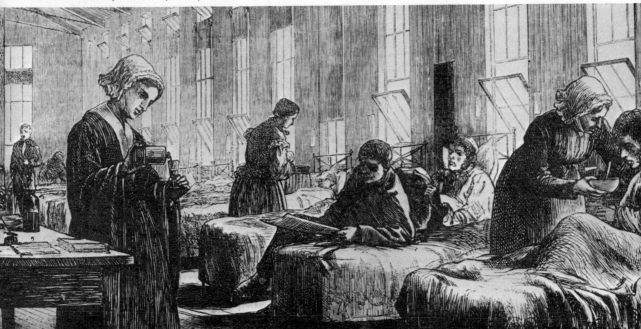

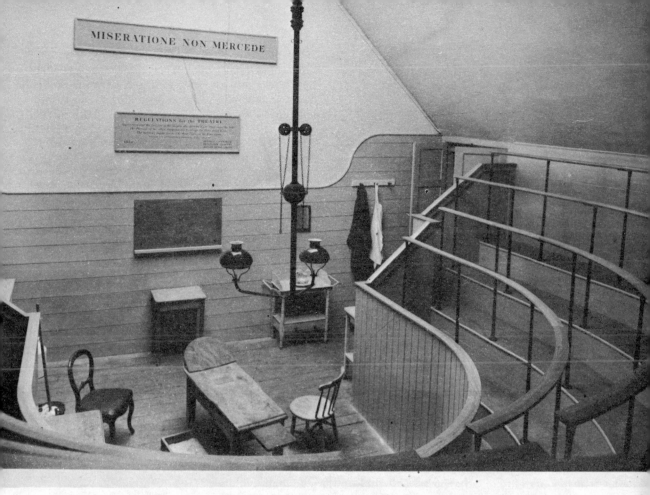

MISERATIONE NON MERCEDE

The operating theatre of old St. Thomas's Hospital, a fine example of an operating theatre of the 1820's. It is now preserved as a museum. Students could watch from the gallery as the surgeons worked on a patient, without anaesthetics of course.

features of the century was the increase in the number of hospitals. The Westminster hospital was founded in 1719. Then in 1725 a London bookseller, Thomas Guy, used money that he had made from the South Sea Bubble to set up the famous hospital that bears his name. By the end of the century there were 11 hospitals in London, 37 outside London and 9 in Scotland.

If the increase in numbers was the encouraging feature of hospital provision, the quality of treatment obtained, and the general conditions endured by the patients was quite the reverse. The first thing a patient entering Bart's did was to deposit a burial fee of nineteen and sixpence, returnable of course in the event of successful treatment. There were maintainance fees in addition to this. Successful treatment was not particularly likely in view of the main principles of treatment, consisting as they did of sweating, purging and bleeding. Bart's used 96 000 leeches in 1837, for instance, to carry out bleeding.

Improvements came slowly, but the pace

increased in the nineteenth century. Special hospitals began to appear, the London Chest Hospital in 1814, the Hospital for Sick Children in 1852. The first child clinic appeared at St. Helens in 1898 and the first convalescent home for physically handicapped children was opened at West Kirby, Merseyside, in 1903.

Some attempt was made to provide free treatment to the 'deserving poor', the Royal Free Hospital being set up in 1828, and after the turn of the century Workhouse hospitals began to improve their standards. In 1929 these hospitals were in fact finally taken over by the local authorities.

Today all hospitals are grouped into fourteen regional areas and provision for hospital building and for making funds available for research etc., now comes from the National Health Service. The cost of hospital provision now rests on the shoulders of every tax and rate payer, and so, in a sense, we all have some say in how much or how little is to be spent on this vital service.

We have already noted how Florence Nightin-

A National Health card which entitles each of us to proper medical attention when we need it. The National Health Service in one of the main features of our Welfare State.

The Prevention of Disease

One must finally remember the politicians and public servants who struggled to cope with disease at its source—the wretched squalor of our towns and cities. Previous chapters have already mentioned most of these, in particular Edwin Chadwick, the man who was the driving force behind the workhouses and was head of the ill-fated Board of Health 1848–1854. He did his best to grapple with the problem of sanitation, the improvement of water supply, the elimination of cholera and tried to make a start on slum clearance.

Disraeli's Home Secretary, Cross, concentrated in his great Public Health Act of 1875 on sewage disposal, slum clearance, the appointment of Medical Officers of Health and Sanitary Inspectors. Later Acts of Parliament have improved standards of purity in food and drugs, water supplies, bathroom provision in older houses etc. In fact all the improvements in these fields charted in Chapter 18 have played their part in the prevention of disease.

One of the prominent features of twentieth century medical advance has been the emphasis placed on its preventitive nature. The School Health Service is an obvious example of this.

gale helped to make nursing an acceptable and honourable career for women. In 1863 there were only 110 paid nurses in the whole of London. At the present day there are over 60 000. Doctors have similarly increased in number. The first issue of the Medical Register in 1859 gave 15 000 registered doctors. The number today is around 90 000.

A modern hospital. The Queen Elizabeth Hospital on the outskirts of Birmingham.

Regular examinations can prevent existing conditions from deteriorating, or better still can destroy some possible danger in infancy. All age groups can benefit from the mobile X-Ray Units which provide an invaluable safeguard against tuberculosis, by giving people the opportunity to have regular checks. Indeed the National Health Service, is preventitive itself, as Chapter 17 made clear, in that fear of a doctor's fee which deterred many from taking medical advice has now gone.

QUESTIONS

1. Make a list of the people mentioned in this chapter and show against each name the reason why they contributed to an advance in medicinal practice.
2. Find out all you can about the hospitals in your area; when they were founded and the scope of the treatment offered.
3. What contributions do central and local government make in looking after your health?

REVISION GUIDES

1 Trades Unions

Trades unions began to appear in the late eighteenth century when workers became simply wage earners in factories and on farms belonging to others. The growth of trades unions coincided with the changeover from domestic to factory industry.

1799. Combination Laws—made trades unions illegal because the Government was afraid they would encourage the spread of revolutionary ideas such as Jacobinism (page 42).

1824. Repeal of the Combination Laws—largely the work of Place and Hume. Led to the immediate outbreak of a number of strikes and the passage of a further law in 1825 making it difficult to strike (page 53).

1829–1834. Attempts to found large general unions of all trades. The most famous attempt was Owen's Grand National Consolidated Trades Union. These efforts failed because they were too ambitious and because the Government took action through Courts e.g. The Tolpuddle Martyrs (page 54).

1851. The establishment of the Amalgamated Society of Engineers—the first craft union to become firmly established. It did not arouse Government opposition because its members were highly skilled craftsmen with a moderate outlook. The A.S.E. operated rather like a Friendly Society (page 79).

1867. The Second Reform Act—gave the vote to working men in the towns and indirectly strengthened the skilled unions like the A.S.E. (page 83).

1868. First Trades Union Congress (page 80).

1869. Royal Commission—reported favourably on the new craft unions and led to *a*) **1871** Trades Disputes Act which protected Union Funds and gave them legal recognition. *b*) **1875** Trades Union Act which allowed peaceful picketing and made it possible to organize effective strikes (page 80).

1889. Successful strike by London dockers—followed by the appearance of unions in many other unskilled trades (page 81).

1901. Taff Vale Judgement—legal decision by the House of Lords forcing a railway union to pay damages following a strike. Seemed to threaten the right of any union to take strike action. Decision reversed by the Trades Disputes Act 1906 (page 89).

1908. Osborne Judgement—House of Lords ruling that union funds could not be used for political purposes. Threatened the financial base of the infant Labour Party. Decision reversed by the Trades Union Act 1913 (page 90).

1921–1926. Period of strikes as unions attempted to fight the effects of the slump following the First World War, culminating in the unsuccessful General Strike of 1926 (page 98).

1927. General Strikes declared illegal by the government (page 100).

1946. Following the election of a Labour Government in 1945 with trades union support, the law making general strikes illegal was repealed.

2 Education

The Industrial Revolution created a need for elementary education for poorer children and also a demand for improved scientific and technical training to meet the requirements of the new 'mechanical age'.

1780. Sunday Schools—established first by Robert Raikes to give basic instruction in reading and writing.

1800 onwards. Increased numbers of church schools set up by the National Society (Church of England) and the British and Foreign Schools Society (Non-conformist). Methods based on the ideas of Lancaster and Bell (page 81).

1833. First state grant to education (page 81).

1858. Royal Commission leads to payment by results (page 81).

1870. Forster's Education Act—state system of elementary education (page 82).

1876. Elementary Education made compulsory (page 82).

1891. Fees for elementary education abolished (page 82).

1902. Balfour Education Act—County and Borough Councils responsible for education, including technical education and the provision of free places in the grammar schools for selected working class children (page 82).

1918. Fisher Education Act—school leaving age raised to 14.

1944. Butler Education Act—free secondary education for all children according to ability. Selection to be made by examination at 11+. School leaving age raised to 15 (pages 108, 110).

1945–1970. Rapid development of further education and the establishment of a large number of new technical colleges and universities. Further changes in the pattern of secondary education leading to the abolition of the 11+ exam. and the spread of comprehensive schools.

3 Factory and Mines Reform

Efforts to reform some of the worst features of the factory system began soon after the Industrial Revolution had started.

1802. The Health and Morals of Apprentices Act—attempted to limit the hours and improve the conditions of the workhouse children who were employed in the early mills. It failed due to the lack of a proper system of inspection (page 47).

1819. Factory Act—attempted to prohibit the employment of all children under 9 and limit the hours of work of those over 9. Also failed due to the lack of a system of inspection (page 47).

1830. Oastler's 'Yorkshire Slavery' articles led to campaign for factory reform leading to: 1833 Factory Act (Shaftesbury). Limited the hours of children working in textile mills as follows:
Under 9—no work at all.
From 9 to 13—9 hour day, 48 hour week.
From 13 to 18—12 hour day, 69 hour week and no night work.
This Act was effective because it appointed Government Inspectors to see that its terms were carried out (page 47).

1842. Mines Act—stated that no women or girls or boys under 10 were to work underground, Government inspectors appointed (page 48).

1844. Factory Act—women classed as young persons and their hours were limited to 12 per day. Hours for children between 9 and 13 reduced to 6½ per day. The act also made provision for the fencing of dangerous machinery (page 48).

1847. Ten Hours Act (Fielden)—Women and boys under 18 to work no more than 10 hours per day. Factory owners began relay working and made it necessary for a further Factory Act to be passed 1850, the 10½ hour 'compromise' (page 48).

1867. Factory Act—extended the factory laws to include industries other than textiles for the first time.

1878. Factories and Workshops Act—stated that no children under 10 to be employed and that children under 14 were to be employed only half a day. This followed the government's decision in 1876 to make elementary education compulsory.

4 Parliamentary Reform

At the beginning of our period political power in this country was in the hands of the landed gentlemen who sat in the House of Lords and packed the House of Commons with their supporters. The social changes brought about by the Industrial Revolution led to demands for reform.

1832. First Reform Act—transferred the seats from the 'rotten', and 'pocket' boroughs to the new industrial towns and larger counties and gave the vote to the new industrial middle class in the towns (page 45).

1867. Second Reform Act—gave the vote to skilled workers in the towns allowing the working class some share in political power for the first time (page 83).

1884. Third Reform Act—gave the vote to almost all adult males in both the towns and the countryside. Triumph of the ideas of democracy (see glossary) (page 84).

1918. Fourth Reform Act—gave the vote to all males over 21 and to women over 30 (page 100).

1928. Fifth Reform Act—gave the vote to women over the age of 21 and completed the process, which had started in 1832, of placing political power in the hands of all the people (page 100).

5 Local Government Reform

Reform of the old system of local government which had grown up in the Middle Ages became necessary following the enormous growth in population and the increase in the number of large towns after the Industrial Revolution.

1835. Municipal Corporations Act—provided for elected councils in the larger towns and gave rate payers the right to vote at local elections (page 50).

1888. County Councils—elected by the rate-payers in country districts, these new County Councils were to administer the counties in the same ways as the town councils had done in urban areas since the reform of 1835 (page 85).

1894. The Counties were sub-divided into smaller units, Urban Districts, Rural Districts, and where necessary into Parishes, each of which was to have an elected council. These smaller councils took over some of the powers of the County Councils for administrative convenience (page 85).

20th. Century. In the present century the powers of the County and Borough Councils have been continually added to so that most matters of local concern are the responsibility of the local council. e.g.

1902—responsibility for education at all levels was transferred to the local authorities who were to form Education Committies.

1907—responsibility for the new school medical service was placed on the local authorities.

1929—the abolition of the old Poor Law system placed responsibility for the administration of the new system of hospitals etc., on the local authorities whose powers were considerably widened as a result (page 100).

GLOSSARY

CAPITALISM
The use of private capital to finance the means of production. The profits from such privately owned businesses are taken by the private individuals who own them or a share of them and capitalism is therefore the opposite of public or collective ownership.

COTTAGE INDUSTRY
Manufacture carried out in peoples own homes. This method of producing goods, sometimes called the Domestic System, was later replaced by factory industry.

COMMUNISM
The application of Socialism to a country by means of a revolution of the working classes as represented by the Communist Party, leading to the state control of all property.

DEMOCRACY
It means 'rule by the people' and usually refers to a system of government which gives people some say in the choice of their rulers by elective means.

DEPRESSION
A Depression or Slump is a serious decline in trade usually accompanied by a fall in prices and profits and an increase in the level of unemployment.

FREE TRADE
Trade is said to be free when all restrictions such as customs duties and import controls are removed, allowing goods to flow freely between one country and another.

INDUSTRIAL REVOLUTION
The term used by historians to describe the changeover from handwork in the home (Cottage Industry) to machine work in factories. In Britain this change began in the second half of the eighteenth century.

LAISSEZ-FAIRE
An absence of government control—literally 'to leave alone'—especially in the realm of industry and commerce, where it was held that trade would flourish best when there was the minimum of government interference.

MONOPOLY
The sole right to manufacture certain goods or provide certain services. Highly successful companies are said to have achieved a monopoly when they have forced their rivals out of business.

POCKET BOROUGH
A borough which returned an M.P. and was situated on the estate of a landowner who could influence the electors by threatening them with eviction or by bringing other pressures to bear. The borough was said to be in the landowner's pocket.

PROTECTION
In the political and economic sense it means the protection of trade by placing duties on imported goods to make them more expensive than similar goods produced in this country. By this means the home producer is protected from foreign competition. Protectionism is the opposite of Free Trade.

ROTTEN BOROUGH

An area which had once been important enough to return an M.P. to Westminster but which by the eighteenth century had decayed to such an extent that it contained hardly any voters. These boroughs and the Parliamentary seats which went with them were bought and sold before 1832.

SOCIALISM

The collective ownership by the community of the means of production (land, factories, mines etc), the means of distribution (road, rail and air transport, shops etc), and the means of exchange (the banks). Profits from this collective ownership are used by the state to finance community services (health schemes, pensions etc).

SUFFRAGETTES

The name given to those who campaigned for women's suffrage i.e. the right of women to vote at Parliamentary elections.

WELFARE STATE

A country which ensures the welfare of all its citizens by providing such benefits as free medical treatment, pensions, insurance and family allowances out of state funds.

TECHNICAL GLOSSARY

CARDING
A process in the textile trade by which short fibres of raw wool and cotton are straightened and separated ready for spinning into yarn. Arkwright patented a carding machine in 1775, six years after the invention of his Water Frame.

COMBING
A process in the textile trade similar to carding by which long fibres of raw wool are straightened and separated from short fibres before being spun into yarn. Long staple wool is used in the manufacture of worsted cloth.

MARLING
The use of good quality soil called marl which consists of a mixture of clay and carbonate of lime to enrich poor quality sandy soil or to act as a fertilizer. Marling is done by spreading marl on the surface of a field or by deep ploughing to raise good quality marly soil to the surface.

NATIONAL GRID
The countrywide network of electrical supplies. Individual power stations manufacture electricity and feed it into the National Grid through which supplies can be distributed to the consumer.

PIG IRON
Iron containing a high proportion of carbon which makes it brittle and suitable only for casting. Wrought iron which contains very little carbon is not brittle can be wrought or worked in a forge into a variety of shapes.

REVERBATORY FURNACE
An iron making furnace in which the flame is reflected from the roof of the kiln onto the iron ore which is being smelted. This avoids direct contact between the iron ore and the fuel being used to fire the furnace and reduces the amount of carbon which is present in the smelted metal.

SHUTTLE
Cigar shaped instrument which carries the weft thread on a loom. The weaver passes the shuttle from side to side through the warp threads attached to the loom in order to weave cloth. This action is called throwing the shuttle.

SOWING SEED BROADCAST
The traditional method of scattering seed by hand. The seed fell in irregular patterns and not in neat rows and was difficult to hoe.

SULPHANILAMIDES
Groups of drugs used to combat diseases and infections caused by minute living organisms called bacteria.

TENTERHOOKS
The hooks used to hold woollen cloth on a tenter or stretching frame. Stretching was one of the finishing processes in the woollen trade and followed the washing of the newly woven cloth after it had come off the loom.

THROWING POTTERY
The action of throwing clay onto a revolving potter's wheel so that it can be shaped by hand. Mass produced pottery is not thrown but manufactured in moulds.

The stationary threads on a loom running lengthways away from the weaver through which the shuttle carrying the weft thread is passed.

The thread on a loom which is attached to the shuttle and is passed or thrown from side to side through the warp in order to make cloth.

INDEX